Foreign Policy

INQUIRY INTO CRUCIAL AMERICAN PROBLEMS

Series Editor · JACK R. FRAENKEL

Foreign Policy:

Intervention, Involvement, or Isolation?

ALVIN WOLF

Social Science Teacher
Westmoor High School
Daly City, California

PRENTICE-HALL, INC.   ENGLEWOOD CLIFFS, N.J.

Titles in this series:

CRIME AND CRIMINALS: What Should We Do About Them?
Jack R. Fraenkel

PREJUDICE AND DISCRIMINATION: Can We Eliminate Them?
Fred R. Holmes

THE DRUG SCENE: Help or Hang-up?
Walter L. Way

POVERTY IN AN AFFLUENT SOCIETY: Personal Problem or National Disgrace?
David A. Durfee

COUNTRY, CONSCIENCE, AND CONSCRIPTION: Can They Be Reconciled?
Leo A. Bressler and Marion A. Bressler

VOICES OF DISSENT: Positive Good or Disruptive Evil?
Frank Kane

CITIES IN CRISIS: Decay or Renewal?
Rudie W. Tretten

TEEN-AGERS AND SEX: Revolution or Reaction?
Jack L. Nelson

PROPAGANDA, POLLS, AND PUBLIC OPINION: Are the People Manipulated?
Malcolm G. Mitchell

ALIENATION: Individual or Social Problem?
Ronald V. Urick

EDUCATION AND OPPORTUNITY: For What and For Whom?
Gordon M. Seely

FOREIGN POLICY: Intervention, Involvement, or Isolation?
Alvin Wolf

ISBN 0-13-326421-1 paper
ISBN 0-13-326439-4 cloth

2 3 4 5 6 7 8 9 10

Prentice-Hall International, Inc.,
London
Prentice-Hall of Australia, Pty. Ltd.,
Sydney
Prentice-Hall of Canada, Ltd.,
Toronto
Prentice-Hall of India Private Ltd.,
New Delhi
Prentice-Hall of Japan, Inc.,
Tokyo

PREFACE

The series *INQUIRY INTO CRUCIAL AMERICAN PROB-LEMS* focuses upon a number of important contemporary social and political issues. Each book presents an in-depth study of a particular problem, selected because of its pressing intrusion into the minds and consciences of most Americans today. A major concern has been the desire to make the materials relevant to students. Every title in the series, therefore, has been selected because, in one way or another, it suggests a problem of concern to students today.

A number of divergent viewpoints, from a wide variety of different *kinds* of sources, encourage discussion and reflection and illustrate that the same problem may be viewed from many different vantage points. Of concern throughout is a desire to help students realize that honest men may legitimately differ in their views.

After a short chapter introducing the questions with which the book will deal, Chapter 2 presents a brief historical and contemporary background so that students will have more than just a superficial understanding of the problem under study. In the readings that follow, a conscientious effort has been made to avoid endorsing any one viewpoint as the "right" viewpoint, or to evaluate the arguments of particular individuals. No conclusions are drawn. Instead, a number of questions for discussion and reflection are posed at the end of each reading so that students can come to their own conclusions.

Great care has been taken to insure that the readings included in each book are just that—readable! We have searched particularly for articles that are of high interest, yet from which differing viewpoints may be legitimately inferred. Whenever possible, dialogues involving or descriptions showing actual people responding and reacting to problematic situations are presented. In sum, each book

- presents divergent, conflicting views on the problem under consideration;

- gives as many perspectives and dimensions on the problem as space permits;

- presents articles on a variety of reading levels, in order to appeal to students of many different ability levels;

- presents analytical as well as descriptive statements;

- deals with real people involved in situations of concern to them;

- includes questions which encourage discussion and thought of the various viewpoints expressed;

- includes activities to involve students to consider further the issues embedded in the problem.

CONTENTS

Introduction

In Peru, a brigadier general leads a successful military revolt, driving a Sherman tank purchased from the United States.

In Honduras, C.I.A. agents organize and help to train Guatemalan troops who eventually cross the border to overthrow the popularly elected Guatemalan government that has earned the disfavor of the United States Government because it contained anti-American Communists.

In Iran, the grandson of a former United States president slips into the capital city of Teheran and, in an action that rivals the fictional exploits of James Bond, succeeds in launching a *coup d'etat* [1] against a government that has threatened to turn vast United States and Western European oil interests over to Russia.

In a short but fierce war, Jordan and Israel fight each other with American tanks.

In Vietnam, an Air Force colonel becomes a leading advisor to a controversial dictator whom the United States is forced later to repudiate, owing to worldwide disgust at the dictator's repressive policies.

In Lebanon, United States Marines land, upon invitation, to protect the existing government from a threatened *coup d'etat*.

In Laos, an American doctor opens a medical center where medical care is badly needed.

---

[1] a sudden overthrow of a government, usually by military means

In a remote part of India, a Peace Corps team of young men and women set up a school.

What do all of these have in common? They are all examples of recent incidents in foreign countries in which the United States has been involved.

For many years, perhaps more so now than in the past, Americans have been asking: Does the United States have a right to become involved in the internal affairs of other nations? A duty? Or should we stick to our own backyard, so to speak, and mend our own fences? Many political commentators argue that the United States does not have such a right or duty. The problem arises when one attempts to define what is meant by "internal affairs," "intervention," "involvement," and "isolation." For example, if someone believes that Fidel Castro is a member of an international conspiracy with its headquarters in Moscow, then he probably believes the "internal affairs" of Cuba have dangerous international implications. This person may feel that it is the duty of the United States to thwart Castro—even to the extent of overthrowing him. On the other hand, if a person believes that Castro is the leader of a popular revolution, who, out of economic necessity, turned to the Soviet Union for aid, then he may believe that the United States should not interfere in Cuban internal affairs. There is no lack of assertions to support either position.

The United States has established a vast military, economic, and political mechanism to prevent the occurrence of Communist take-overs in other countries. There are over one million armed forces personnel stationed abroad at far-flung outposts—from West Germany to South Korea, from Ethiopia to Vietnam—whose commitment is the containment of communism to its present frontiers. The United States is the principal power in three separate alliance systems that protect thirty nations from external aggression as well as—at times—internal subversion. Bilateral arms agreements exist with many countries, including at times such mutual antagonists as India and Pakistan, and Jordan and Israel. Since World War II, the United States has extended over $110 billion worth of foreign aid to nations as diverse as England, Laos, and Yugoslavia. Through the C.I.A. the United States has overthrown one government hostile to her purposes, failed in an attempt to overthrow another, and helped maintain governments that are friendly. Through the Peace Corps, the United States has attempted to educate as well as to become acquainted with the people of other cultures. The United States, using troops, foreign aid, the C.I.A., the Peace Corps, public agencies, and private corporations, has become "involved" in the affairs of nearly all the nations of the world in the past twenty years. And this, of course, in addition to participating in the United Nations.

You may have already perceived that the involvement of one nation in the affairs of another can take many forms. This book will consider some examples of economic, political, military, and humanitarian involvement. Sometimes it is the *government* of one nation that becomes involved in another country's affairs; at other times it is a private company or an individual acting independently of his government. Both kinds of involvement, government and private, are illustrated in this book.

As you read further, you will have the opportunity to analyze a number of statements to determine when, or whether, it is proper for the United States, or any country, to intervene, or interfere, or become involved in the affairs of another country. You should also consider such questions as these:

1. What does "involvement in the affairs of another country" mean?
2. Are there varying degrees of involvement?
3. What causes a nation to become involved in another country's affairs?
4. What are the effects of foreign intervention or foreign investment on the nations concerned?
5. What alternatives to involvement exist?
6. When, if ever, is involvement justified?
7. Is isolation possible in today's world?

Foreign Policy: Past Involvements

To what extent has foreign involvement been a part of America's history? When has the United States intervened in another nation's affairs? To what extent? Why? With what results? Is such a policy necessary today? Justified? This chapter presents some examples of America's relations with other nations in the past.

FRENCH INVOLVEMENT IN THE AMERICAN REVOLUTION

French military and economic aid in the Revolutionary War helped America win her independence. Shortly before the American colonies declared themselves freed from England, French money and supplies secretly found their way to the American cause. "About 90 per cent of all the gunpowder used by the Americans in the first two and a half years of the [Revolutionary] war came from French arsenals." [1] Two years later, in 1778, France threw off the wraps from her aid program and through a treaty of alliance against Britain, openly joined America in the latter's war for independence.

As a consequence of this treaty France played a major role in Britain's quitting the war and recognizing her former colonies' independence. The last main battle of the war ended on October 19, 1781, when Britain's Lord Cornwallis surrendered 7,000 men to George Washington. The trap that closed around Cornwallis at Yorktown peninsula consisted of one American army, Washington's, and one French army, under the Comte de Rochambeau. Admiral de Grasse's French fleet closed the trap from the seaward side. Cornwallis could not get out. "The triumph," says Professor Thomas Bailey, "was no less a French victory

---

[1] Thomas Bailey, *The American Pageant,* p. 114

4

than an American one: The French provided essentially all the seapower and about half the regular troops in the besieging army of some 16,000 men." [2]

NO ENTANGLING ALLIANCES

Not too long after securing independence, the United States had her first opportunity to become engaged militarily in another country's affairs.

In 1792, the Wars of the French Revolution began. The two major antagonists, Britain and France, fought until 1815. American public opinion was divided about the war. Some Americans looked upon the French revolutionists and their announced goal of "Liberty, Equality, Fraternity" as being inspired by the American Revolution. Others were pro-British for economic or sentimental reasons, or because they opposed the guillotine methods used by the radical revolutionists in France to eliminate their political opponents. France, in her time of need, expected the United States to aid her, as called for in the mutual aid alliance of 1778. Both antagonists tried to prevent American ships from sailing to each other's ports. Despite the Treaty and sentiments for both sides in America, the Washington Administration proclaimed neutrality.

America's republican representative democracy was small and struggling for survival in a hostile world of dictatorial monarchies. At home political divisions and economic problems were plentiful. There were British army posts on the Great Lakes and intrigues to split off the west to form a new country with Spain's North American territories. Precarious relationships with the Indians threatened the frontier. The young nation had enough to do to put her own house in order. She couldn't enjoy the luxury of meddling in the affairs of others.

In his Farewell Address, President Washington counseled Americans not to become involved in other countries' problems, if it were not in America's interests to do so. He warned:

The great rule of conduct for us in regard to foreign nations is, in extending our commercial relations to have with them as little *political* connection as possible. . . . It is our true policy to steer clear of permanent alliances with any portion of the foreign world. . . . Taking care always to keep ourselves by suitable establishments on a respectable defensive posture, we may safely trust to temporary alliances for extraordinary emergencies.[3]

Four years later, in his first inaugural address, Thomas Jefferson pledged his administration to a policy of no entangling alliances.

The cornerstone of American foreign policy was laid. America would

---

[2] *ibid.*, p. 121
[3] James Richardson, *A Compilation of the Messages and Papers of the Presidents,* New York, N. Y.: Bureau of National Literature, 1897.

not again commit itself to a mutual aid agreement until 1948. In the meantime, however, there were many occasions when it appeared to be in the national interest to become involved in other countries' affairs.

THE MONROE DOCTRINE

Through the Monroe Doctrine the United States began a policy of political involvement in Latin American affairs, to protect the countries of the Western Hemisphere from outside interference.

The Wars of the French Revolution had ended in 1815. Except for Britain, dictatorial monarchies reigned in the major countries of Europe. But the spirit of the American and French revolutions had reached Latin America. Taking advantage of Spain's and Portugal's involvement in the European wars, the Latin Americans declared their independence from these two major colonial powers. Four European monarchies, led by France and Austria, schemed to form a "Quadruple Alliance" to regain the lost colonies for Spain and Portugal. If the Alliance were successful, the independence of the United States might be threatened. The Monroe Doctrine proclaimed the United States to be the protector of Latin America.

In the wars of the European powers in matter relating to themselves we have never taken any part, nor does it comport with our policy so to do. It is only when our rights are invaded or seriously menaced that we resent injuries or make preparation for our defense. With the movements in this hemisphere we are of necessity more immediately connected . . . We . . . declare that we should consider any attempt on their part (European powers) to extend their system to any portion of this hemisphere as dangerous to our peace and safety. With the existing colonies or dependencies of any European power we have not interfered and shall not interfere. But with the Governments who have declared their independence and maintained it . . . we could not view any interposition [4] for the purpose of oppressing them, or controlling in any other manner their destiny, by any European power in any other light than as the manifestation of an unfriendly disposition toward the United States. . . . It is impossible that the allied powers should extend their political system to any portion of . . . (the western hemisphere) without endangering our peace and happiness. . . .[5]

Between 1823 and 1898 the United States invoked the Monroe Doctrine on three significant occasions, to involve itself politically in the affairs of Latin America. President Polk issued his corollary to the Doctrine in 1848 when it was rumored that the local rulers of the Yucatan Peninsula,

---

[4] intervention
[5] *ibid.,* II, pp. 778–788

Mexico, were going to offer their area to Britain. The nearby Panamanian isthmus was vital to quick passage across the American continents. The United States did not want that passageway threatened by the presence of a non-American power. President Polk announced that the United States would not permit such a transfer of territory even with the consent of the people involved.

During the Civil War the Monroe Doctrine was invoked against French military forces that had overthrown the republican government of Mexico and were supporting the new monarchy of the Austrian Archduke Ferdinand Maximilian. In 1864 the House of Representatives resolved by a vote of 109–0 that

. . . The Congress of the United States are unwilling by silence to leave the nations of the world under the impression that they are indifferent spectators of the deplorable events now transpiring in the republic of Mexico, and that they therefore think fit to declare that it does not accord with the policy of the United States to acknowledge any monarchial Government erected on the ruins of any republican Government in America under the auspices of any European Power.[6]

The United States reached a new height of self-assertion in 1895 when, upon Venezuela's request, it urged Britain to accept arbitration as the means to solve a border dispute between Venezuela and British Guiana. To pressure Britain, President Grover Cleveland, backed by jingoist[7] elements, indicated that war might be used to move Britain to the negotiating table. In what the British foreign office considered a haughty and unfounded interpretation of the Monroe Doctrine, Secretary of State Richard Olney proclaimed:

To-day the United States is practically sovereign on this continent, and its fiat is law upon the subjects to which it confines its interposition. Why? It is not . . . because wisdom and justice and equity are the invariable characteristics of the dealings of the United States. It is because, in addition to all other grounds, its infinite resources combined with its isolated position render it master of the situation and practically invulnerable as against any or all other powers.[8]

THE WAR WITH SPAIN, 1898, AND THE "OPEN DOOR" NOTES

Starting with the Spanish-American War of 1898, and continuing through the 1920's, America became involved militarily, politically, and economically in the affairs of many Latin American republics. The imme-

---

[6] Thomas Bailey, *A Diplomatic History of the American People,* New York: Appleton-Century-Crofts, Inc., 6th Edition, 1958.
[7] superpatriotic
[8] *ibid.,* p. 441

diate pretext for intervening militarily in Cuba in 1898 was the sinking of the battleship *Maine* in Havana harbor. Though no one ever proved that the Spanish were responsible for this deed, the American people were willing to believe that it was so, owing to the long campaign that the Hearst and Pulitzer newspapers had carried on since 1895 against Spanish "atrocities" in Cuba. Americans sympathized with the struggling "underdog" Cubans who wanted independence. Another factor was the economic depression in the United States in the 1890's; many businessmen felt the stern necessity of attaining new markets abroad to supply an outlet for the manufactured goods of which, for the first time in her history, America was producing a surplus. Albert J. Beveridge, one of the foremost proponents of American expansion abroad, spoke for many in 1897: "American factories are making more than the American people can use. American soil is producing more than they can consume. Fate has written our policy for us; the trade of the world must and shall be ours."

The Americans waged a successful war against a decrepit Spanish fleet and a hopelessly backward Spanish army in 1898. The real problems of empire, however, began only after the war was over. Should America annex Cuba and the Philippines—the spoils of war? Would this not contradict the American doctrine of self-determination for all nations? The United States, after all, had justified its intervention in Cuba and the Philippines largely on the ground that the Spaniards were cruel and oppressive overlords. But in 1898, these subject peoples had been waging their *own* war against the Spaniards, and there was no certainty that in the end they could not have liberated themselves without the military might of America.

On the issue of the annexation of the Philippines, vigorous debate arose in America between "imperialists" and "anti-imperialists." Despite the opposition, the United States annexed the Philippines. The booty from the Spanish-American War, however, helped bring about so much internal dissension that the United States never again embarked upon a policy of colonialism. Instead, in the years after the war with Spain, it evolved the ingenious Open Door Policy, as an alternative to territorial expansion in Asia. Through a series of three communications, known as the "Open Door Notes," to various European powers, the United States insisted upon the freedom to engage in trade at all European-controlled ports in Asia. The United States did not wish to see China carved up into separate "spheres of influence," but insisted upon the right to deal with Chinese officials on matters of trade and industrial development. Here was a form of political pressure to safeguard American economic interests.

INCREASED CONTROL OF THE WESTERN HEMISPHERE

Victory over Spain also opened an intensified interest in Latin America for the United States. The Caribbean was to become a lake of the "Colossus of the North." Cuba, freed from Spanish rule to become independent, remained under American rule until 1903, when it was deemed ready for independence. However, as a condition of independence, Cuba had to accept the Platt Amendment, which allowed the United States to intervene, when the latter judged it necessary, to preserve internal order and independence, and to lease or sell to the United States sites for naval bases.

In the early years of the Twentieth Century some Latin American republics suffered from civil disorder and financial irresponsibility. In some countries the lives and property of Europeans were in jeopardy. Some debts owed to European creditors went unpaid. Germany, Italy, and Britain were ready to use military force to collect their due and protect their people. President Theodore Roosevelt considered the complaints legitimate; the contemplated action was understandable. But the Monroe Doctrine and North American interests in Latin America would not permit European interference. How, then, to do justice to the Europeans, without endangering America's interests? The Roosevelt Corollary to the Monroe Doctrine made the United States the policeman of the western hemisphere. In his annual message to the Congress in December, 1904, the President announced:

If a nation shows that it knows how to act with reasonable efficiency and decency in social and political matters, if it keeps order and pays its obligations, it need fear no interference from the United States. Chronic wrongdoing . . . may in America, as elsewhere, ultimately require intervention by some civilized nation, and in the Western Hemisphere the adherence of the United States to the Monroe Doctrine may force the United States, however reluctantly, in flagrant cases of such wrongdoing or impotence, to the exercise of an international police power.[9]

The Big Stick Policy was born. For three decades United States military forces would be used to discipline Latin American governments and also protect North American economic investments.

THE PROTECTOR BECOMES A "GOOD NEIGHBOR"

In 1928 President-elect Herbert Hoover tried to counter the effect of the Roosevelt Corollary by embarking on a goodwill tour of Latin America. A Cuban journalist of the time outlined what the United States had to do to establish the goodwill Hoover sought.

If Mr. Hoover wants to conquer the immediate sympathy of Latin America, he should at once announce a change in the policy of his country, declaring that the Monroe Doctrine does not mean that the

---

[9] James Richardson, *A Compilation of the Messages and Papers of the Presidents,* New York, N. Y.: Bureau of National Literature, 1897.

American continent is only for the United States, that Haiti will be evacuated, that Nicaragua shall be freed from foreign yoke, that Cuba will see the quick abrogation of the Platt Amendment, that our commercial treaties will cease being one-sided affairs, that our countries will be free to manage their own affairs as they deem fit, and yet that the United States is a real friend in fact, and not a conqueror.[10]

In the 1930's the United States backed away from the Big Stick Policy. Military forces were withdrawn from Haiti and Nicaragua. No longer would the "Colossus of the North" become involved unilaterally in the domestic quarrels of the Latin American republics. Franklin Roosevelt's Good Neighbor Policy reinterpreted the Monroe Doctrine to mean that the United States was no longer the policeman of her sister republics' behavior and that the prohibition against European interference in the western hemisphere was no longer to be unilaterally enforced, but multilaterally.

TWO WORLD WARS DRAW AMERICA'S ATTENTION TO EUROPE

The United States became economically and sentimentally involved in what was to become World War I before she became a belligerent. Shortly after war broke out in Europe in August, 1914, President Woodrow Wilson urged the American people to be "neutral in thought as well as in deed." Many Americans found it difficult to heed the President's advice. Some American financial interests had large investments in Britain, which might have been jeopardized if the latter were to lose the war. Far more trade was carried on with Britain and France than with their enemy, Germany. American democracy was identified with the British and French democracies, not with the German autocracy. American culture was more an emulation of British culture than of any other. On the whole, outspoken Americans were not neutral, but showed favoritism toward Britain. Americans sailed to western Europe, not to central Europe, on British and French ships, not German. German submarine attacks upon these ships, endangering American lives, finally reached a level that caused the United States to abandon her official state of neutrality, and she joined the war against Germany.

What was to become World War II started in Europe twenty-one years after World War I ended. Once again the United States was a self-proclaimed neutral. But during that two year period before she became a belligerent, America was politically and somewhat militarily involved.

By the summer of 1940 Nazi Germany was in control of the European continent west of Russia. Great Britain was the only democracy

---

[10] *Literary Digest,* December 8, 1928.

standing between the United States and the expanding aims of Adolf Hitler. Though "officially" neutral, the United States aided Hitler's enemies. Fifty destroyers were turned over to Britain in exchange for naval and air bases on Britain's western hemispheric possessions, ranging from Newfoundland to the Caribbean. Through Lend-Lease, any country fighting Hitler was eligible to receive war supplies from the United States. By late 1941 American ships trailed German submarines and reported their locations to Britain's navy. Denmark's Greenland was taken over to prevent Germany's acquisition of that strategic island. British, American, and other neutrals' ships were escorted by the U. S. Navy to Iceland, where the Royal Navy picked them up and escorted them to Britain. Thus neutral America participated in Europe's war.

"CONTAINMENT" OF COMMUNISM

It was after World War II that American involvement in other countries' affairs, mainly political and military, though with some humanitarian aspects, reached its highest level.

Unfortunately, the dream of a united world dedicated to peace and cooperation that was supposed to come out of World War II was not yet to be. By 1947 an "Iron Curtain" had fallen over Eastern Europe, as Russia established her satellite states. Communist guerrillas challenged the constitutional monarchy of Greece. Russia tried to secure military positions in Turkey through diplomatic pressure. Communist candidates, capitalizing on Western Europe's economic miseries, stood a good chance of winning elections. In China communist forces swept out the nationalist leader, Chiang Kai-shek. In 1950 Russian-supported North Korea invaded American-backed South Korea. During the ensuing decade nationalist forces (often communist supported) made efforts to throw off what they considered to be oppressive governments in Guatemala, Vietnam, the Dominican Republic, and Cuba. Russia and Red China supported and encouraged internal restlessness in Africa, Latin America, and the Near East. How was the United States to react to what it believed was a danger not only to the peace and stability of the world but also to the safety and security of its own interests?

Traditionally, as we have seen, America's foreign policy had been one of no entangling alliances or involvement unless American interests were concerned. This had meant United States forces venturing into Latin America, diplomatic maneuverings to maintain the Open Door Policy, and economic and military aid to support democratic Britain in her wars against Germany's expanding autocracy. It was hoped that colonialism would be a thing of the past after World War II. This ideal, however, was not so easily attained. In many places, communist forces supported aspirations of nationalist, anti-colonial forces. Many colonies belonged to some of America's friends—Britain, France, Belgium, and Holland.

The program by which the United States would try to prevent the spread of international communism was called *containment.* Wherever communism would try to expand, the United States would move to block it. Containment consisted of military aid, economic aid, and mutual defense pacts. Taking the world by regions, the program consisted of the following:

A.   In Europe:

1.   The Truman Doctrine: It became the "policy of the United States to support free peoples who are resisting attempted subjugation by armed minorities or by outside pressures" by giving their governments economic and military aid. The first assistance, $400 million worth, went to Greece and Turkey.

2.   The Marshall Plan: The European nations were to join together to devise plans for economic recovery from the destruction of World War II. They were to determine to what extent they could help themselves and each other and then inform the United States about their unfulfilled needs. The United States would give them whatever financial assistance it could. Over a three year period, a $10.25 billion "economic blood transfusion" stimulated Western Europe's economy to recovery. The westward surge of communism was stopped.

3.   The North Atlantic Treaty Organization (NATO): A mutual defense pact among the United States, Canada, Britain, France, Italy, Belgium, Iceland, Holland, Denmark, Luxembourg, Portugal, and Norway. Later, Greece and Turkey joined. Not since 1778 had the United States committed herself to aid specific nations if they were the victims of aggression. In a separate agreement the United States pledged to defend the Federal Republic of West Germany. There are today several hundred thousand American military men stationed throughout Europe. A powerful battle fleet patrols the Mediterranean Sea.

B.   In Asia:

1.   A series of pacts were made with Japan, the Philippines, Australia, and New Zealand to consult for defense purposes. The United States negotiated for military bases in Japan and the Philippines. In 1954 the South East Asia Treaty Organization (SEATO) created a community whereby in the event of aggression or subversion the members would "consult immediately" for defense purposes. The members included the United States, Britain, France, Australia, New Zealand, the Philippines, Thailand, and Pakistan.

2.   From 1950–1953, under the United Nations flag, United States military forces assisted South Korea in repelling North Korean aggression. (Thirty-three thousand Americans died in this "police action.") Today, United States forces are still in Korea to advise and assist the Army of South Korea.

3.   The United States maintains bases on Nationalist Chinese

Formosa, in South Korea, the Philippines, and Japan, and on occupied Okinawa. The latter may eventually be returned to Japan, with an agreement to leave the American bases there. A large battle fleet patrols the water of the Orient.

4.   In South Vietnam the United States has maintained military forces, sometimes mounting to over a half million men, since 1954, in helping that government to prevent a communist takeover. Tens of thousands of Americans have died in this war. In 1964 President Johnson proclaimed that no Asian government's request for American aid against a communist threat to its existence would be denied.

C.   In The Middle East:

1.   In 1954 the Middle East Treaty Organization tied Turkey, Iraq, Iran, Pakistan, and Great Britain into a mutual defense relationship. The United States did not join, but worked with this group.

2.   In 1957, President Dwight D. Eisenhower announced his doctrine that the United States would come to the aid of any Middle Eastern nation threatened by communist interference.

D.   In Latin America:

1.   The Organization of American States (O.A.S.) is a regional United Nations. The United States and the Latin American republics have agreed to resolve their grievances through negotiations, and to protect each other from external aggression and subversion, whether from within or outside the western hemisphere.

2.   The Alliance For Progress: A Latin America "Marshall Plan" to develop a modern and prosperous economy in Latin America. The program continues at a slower and less successful pace than did the Marshall Plan for Europe.

E.   Worldwide economic and military aid is still provided to countries that the United States finds it in her interest to help. These include such diverse governments as the communist Tito's in Yugoslavia and right-wing dictatorships in Latin America and Spain.

F.   In underdeveloped areas of Africa, Asia, and Latin America, the Peace Corps, since 1961, has sent thousands of people to so-called backward areas to work as teachers, engineers of various sorts, doctors, farm advisers, and consultants in economic and social development in an effort to wipe out disease, famine, poverty, and ignorance.

G.   In addition to the efforts mentioned above, the United States has engaged in various clandestine operations. For example, in 1954, agents from the United States Central Intelligence Agency helped bring about the overthrow of a pro-Communist government in Guatemala. The C.I.A. has also been involved in other attempts to assist governments struggling against communism. Some of these efforts will be described later on.

In summary, after many changes in the extent of our involvement in world affairs, the United States is at present committed to a wide variety of pacts and programs to defend the national self-interest and to protect the democratic ideal. The chapters that follow will explore some of these various forms of involvement—political, economic, and humanitarian—and examine some possibilities for the future role of the United States on the international scene.

What Do You Think?

1. How would you define involvement at this point?
2. What arguments could you offer *against* involvement at this time?

3

Military Involvement

In 1954 French colonial rule came to an end in what was then called Indo-China. Through an agreement made at Geneva between the Indo-Chinese and the French, three independent states were created in the area—Laos, Cambodia, and Vietnam. The latter was to be temporarily divided at the 17th parallel. The communist forces, which fought the French, dominated in the North. In the South non-communist forces, which also fought the French, prevailed. The Geneva agreement specified that in 1956, after both parts of Vietnam had settled down, elections were to be held to unify the country under one government. Conceivably, that government could well have been a coalition of communists and non-communists. The elections were not held as scheduled.

The Prime Minister of South Vietnam, Ngo Dinh Diem, faced much opposition. Buddhist sects accused him of using police state tactics against them when they complained about their lack of a proportionate voice in the government. He was also accused of corruption and favoritism, while large numbers of people suffered from poverty. Many of his critics were imprisoned. There apparently was a strong likelihood that Diem would lose in a free, fair election in 1956. His opponents complained that fear of losing prompted Diem not to hold the election as prescribed. Diem explained that the communists in the North would not allow a free, fair election but would manipulate it so they would win.

Anti-Diem forces in the South, denied the satisfaction they anticipated from an election, went into rebellion against the Prime Minister. Some were communists and some were not. Whether the communists were supplied from the North, and indeed, whether some of the rebels were North Vietnamese, has been a widely debated question. Diem labeled the insurrectionists as communists. He asked the United States to aid his non-communist government.

Commencing in 1956, a small group of American technical, political, and military advisers were sent to Vietnam to solidify the Diem Government's hold in the countryside, to develop the economy, and to train and advise the military. Between 1956 and 1964 the number of advisers grew gradually. American soldiers in the country were not to engage in any fighting at first. But when they went on patrols with the Army of South Vietnam, they came under fire. Subsequent orders allowed them to fight in self-defense. By 1964 many were engaged in offensive actions against the communists.

The enemy in Vietnam consisted of two groups: the National Liberation Front (N.L.F.), commonly called the Viet Cong, guerrillas from the northern as well as the southern part of the country. It was difficult to catch these guerrillas, as they blended in with the populace of the villages. The Army of North Vietnam was also in the fight by 1964.

1964 was a pivotal year in the war. It was the beginning of an escalation of forces that was to culminate in 1968, when the total number of American troops in Vietnam reached 540,000. The troop build-ups came about after North Vietnamese torpedo boats allegedly attacked American destroyers in the Gulf of Tonkin in August, 1964. The United States retaliated by bombing coastal targets in North Vietnam, and Congress approved President Lyndon Johnson's request that he might take whatever action he thought necessary to protect American lives and military property in Vietnam. When attacks against American bases followed, the President sent more troops and air power to assist the South Vietnamese Army. Warplanes bombed the North's industrial cities, which were suspected of providing war equipment, and the support-lines—trails—in the North, in the South, and in Laos, over which came supplies for the anti-government forces.

Land fighting in Vietnam was confined to the South, while bombing occurred in both the North and South. Much destruction and suffering occurred in the North, the results of the bombings. Huge bombs from high flying B-52 bombers; napalm bombs, rockets, and machine guns from fighter-bombers; and the weapons of land troops and riverboat sailors destroyed many lives and much property in the South.

By 1969 public debate was intense. Proponents of the war argued, basically, that the war was being fought to stop communist expansion in Asia. Opponents spoke of the suffering and destruction in Vietnam, the neglect of serious domestic problems within the

United States, and the continuation of police-state tactics by the Government of the South against its political opponents.

The articles which follow present a number of views on the nature of American involvement in Vietnam.

1. SHOULD THE UNITED STATES HAVE INTERVENED? YES!

Former Secretary of Defense Robert McNamara was one of the chief advisers to Presidents Kennedy and Johnson on the Vietnam War. He and many other leaders in government were convinced that America had to send troops to fight in that war. What were their reasons?

Robert McNamara Responds to Communist Aggression *

According to McNamara, what would have happened if America had not sent her troops into Vietnam?

I turn now to a consideration of United States' objectives in South Viet-Nam. The United States has no designs whatever on the resources or territory of the area. Our national interests do not require that South Viet-Nam serve as a Western base or as a member of a Western Alliance.

Our concern is three-fold.

First, and most important, is the simple fact that South Viet-Nam, a member of the free-world family, is striving to preserve its independence from Communist attack. The Vietnamese have asked our help. We have given it. We shall continue to give it.

We do so in their interest; and we do so in our own clear self-interest. For basic to the principles of freedom and self-determination which have sustained our country for almost two centuries is the right of peoples everywhere to live and develop in peace. Our own security is strengthened by the determination of others to remain free, and by our commitment to assist them. We will not let this member of our family down, regardless of its distance from our shores.

The ultimate goal of the United States in Southeast Asia, as in the rest of the world, is to help maintain free and independent nations which can develop politically, economically, and socially, and which can be responsible members of the world Community. In this region and else-where, many peoples share our sense of the value of such freedom and independence. They have taken the risks and made the sacrifices linked to

---

* Excerpted from Marcus Raskin and Bernard Fall, eds. *The Vietnam Reader,* New York: Random House, 1965. Reprinted by permission of Random House, Inc.

the commitment to membership in the family of the free world. They have done this in the belief that we would back up our pledges to help defend them. It is not right or even expedient—nor is it in our nature—to abandon them when the going is difficult.

Second, Southeast Asia has great strategic significance in the forward defense of the United States. Its location across east-west air and sea lanes flanks the Indian subcontinent on one side and Australia, New Zealand, and the Philippines on the other, and dominates the gateway between the Pacific and Indian Oceans. In Communist hands, this area would pose a most serious threat to the security of the U. S. and to the family of free-world nations to which we belong. To defend Southeast Asia, we must meet the challenge in South Viet-Nam.

And third, South Viet-Nam is a test case for the new Communist strategy. Let me examine for a moment the nature of this strategy.

Just as the Kennedy Administration was coming into office in January, 1961, Chairman Khrushchev made one of the most important speeches on Communist strategy of recent decades. In his report on a Party conference entitled "For New Victories of the World Communist Movement," Khrushchev stated: "In modern conditions, the following categories of wars should be distinguished: world wars, local wars, liberation wars and popular uprisings." He ruled out what he called "world wars" and "local wars" as being too dangerous for profitable indulgence in a world of nuclear weapons. But with regard to what he called "liberation wars," he referred specifically to Viet-Nam. He said, "It is a sacred war. We recognize such wars. . . ."

Communist interest in insurgency techniques did not begin with Khrushchev, nor for that matter with Stalin. Lenin's works are full of tactical instructions, which were adapted very successfully by Mao Tse-tung, whose many writings on guerrilla warfare have become classic references. Indeed, Mao claims to be the true heir of Lenin's original prescriptions for the worldwide victory of Communism. The North Vietnamese have taken a leaf or two from Mao's book—as well as Moscow's—and added some of their own.

Thus today in Viet-Nam we are not dealing with factional disputes or the remnants of a colonial struggle against the French, but rather with a major test case of Communism's new strategy. That strategy has so far been pursued in Cuba, may be beginning in Africa, and failed in Malaya and the Philippines only because of a long and arduous struggle by the people of these countries with assistance provided by the British and the U. S.

In Southeast Asia, the Communists have taken full advantage of geography—the proximity to the Communist base of operations and the rugged, remote, and heavily foliated character of the border regions. They have utilized the diverse ethnic, religious, and tribal groupings, and exploited factionalism and legitimate aspirations wherever possible. And, as I said earlier, they have resorted to sabotage, terrorism, and assassination on an unprecedented scale.

Who is the responsible party—the prime aggressor? First and foremost, without doubt, the prime aggressor is North Viet-Nam, whose leadership has explicitly undertaken to destroy the independence of the South. To be sure, Hanoi is encouraged on its aggressive course by Communist China. But Peiping's interest is hardly the same as that of Hanoi.

For Hanoi, the immediate objective is limited: conquest of the South and national unification, perhaps coupled with control of Laos. For Peiping, however, Hanoi's victory would be only a first step toward eventual Chinese hegemony [1] over the two Viet-Nams and Southeast Asia, and towards exploitation of the new strategy in other parts of the world.

Communist China's interests are clear: It has publicly castigated Moscow for betraying the revolutionary cause whenever the Soviets have sounded a cautionary note. It has characterized the United States as a paper tiger and has insisted that the revolutionary struggle for "liberation and unification" of Viet-Nam could be conducted without risks by, in effect, crawling under the nuclear and the conventional defense of the free world. Peiping thus appears to feel that it has a large stake in demonstrating the new strategy, using Viet-Nam as a test case. Success in Viet-Nam would be regarded by Peiping as vindication for China's views in the worldwide ideological struggle.

Taking into account the relationship of Viet-Nam to Indochina—and of both to Southeast Asia, the Far East and the free world as a whole— five U. S. Presidents have acted to preserve free-world strategic interests in the area. President Roosevelt opposed Japanese penetration in Indochina; President Truman resisted Communist aggression in Korea; President Eisenhower backed Diem's efforts to save South Viet-Nam and undertook to defend Taiwan; President Kennedy stepped up our counterinsurgency effort in Viet-Nam; and President Johnson, in addition to reaffirming . . . that the United States will furnish assistance and support to South Viet-Nam for as long as it is required to bring Communist aggression and terrorism under control, has approved the program . . .

The U. S. role in South Viet-Nam, then, is: *first,* to answer the call of the South Vietnamese, a member nation of our free-world family, to help them save their country for themselves; *second,* to help prevent the strategic danger which would exist if Communism absorbed Southeast Asia's people and resources; and third, to prove in the Vietnamese test case that the free world can cope with Communist "wars of liberation" as we have coped successfully with Communist aggression at other levels.

---

[1] leadership

What Do You Think?

1.   Secretary McNamara states that many countries have made sacrifices and taken risks to remain free countries believing that the United States would back them up. Should the United States pledge to help such countries to defend themselves?
2.   Is there any way, other than the use of American troops, to stop communist insurgency in other countries? What would you suggest?

What Now in Vietnam? *

The National Review *is a magazine that has expressed strong support for America's presence in Vietnam. It believes American troops must remain there until the Viet Cong and the North Vietnamese army are militarily defeated. Why should the United States intervene in such situations? The* National Review *argues as follows;*

National Review has consistently supported American intervention in Vietnam, although it has often been critical of the conduct and methods of the intervention.

· American security and interest, understood in the given strategic and political context, required intervention. The advance of Communist power into Southeast Asia would inevitably mean a transformation, to the major detriment of American security and interest, of the strategic, political and economic equilibrium of the Southeast Asian peninsula, the larger western Pacific area and the Indian subcontinent. This would be the consequence no matter what the precise relation of the local Communism to the major centers of Communist power.

· The Communist advance would mean the smashing of our forward strategic defense line, forcing a pullback to our own Pacific shore, with Hawaii becoming an exposed outpost.

· It would put control of the Pacific and global sea routes and critical global airways into Communist hands.

· It would, as in the case of the Communist conquest of Eastern Europe, prevent fruitful development of trade and economic relations with the region.

· It would compel all the nations of the region—Japan, Indonesia, the Philippine Republic, Pakistan and India, as well as the Southeast Asian

* Excerpted from "What Now in Vietnam?" *National Review,* May 6, 1969.
National Review, Inc., 150 East 35th St., N. Y., N. Y. 10016

nations—either to submit to outright Communist rule or to adjust their regimes to the reality of Communist hegemony.

· It would weaken the prestige, credibility and influence of the United States in all the rest of the world.

· If the Communist advance was to be stopped, it had to be stopped somewhere. . . .

· [T]he nature of the Communist aggression in Vietnam, initiated and commanded by Communist North Vietnam and supplied from other external Communist centers, made intervention politically compelling. Failure to intervene in South Vietnam would only have postponed the decision a few years until the identical issue would have been posed in relation to mounting attacks in Thailand, Malaysia or India, under conditions that would have become much worse from both military and political standpoints.

· Intervention was also called for politically and morally, by a long line of American statements, declarations and assurances, and by the intrinsic nature of the Vietnam situation. There was and is no question of what Communist takeover would mean to the people of South Vietnam. When the Communists won in North Vietnam, several hundred thousand persons were executed and nearly two million fled south. By 1965 (when massive American intervention began) Communist terrorists had already executed tens of thousands of persons in the south, chiefly in the villages. Communist rule in South Vietnam, in the process of imposing totalitarian despotism, would carry through a mass slaughter on a larger scale than in the north, since so many in the south, starting with the two million refugees, the soldiers and the governmental service, are plainly marked as opposed to Communism. To have refused to give South Vietnam the support which it needed and asked would have been an abandonment of any claim to leadership in the free world. It would have been in paralyzing contrast with the powerful support furnished to North Vietnam by both China and the Soviet Union.

*   *   *   *   *

· American military intervention in 1965 halted the Communist victory which, without the intervention, was only a few months off.

· Whatever questions there may be about what exactly has happened since then in South Vietnam, there is no doubt that:

· The Communists control considerably less of the area and population than in 1965.

· The Communists have little influence in the cities.

· The North Vietnamese-Vietcong forces have suffered grievous attrition.

· The South Vietnamese army is stronger and more cohesive than it has ever been, and increasingly so.

· The South Vietnamese government, on the foundation of the improved military situation, is increasingly representative, confident and responsible.

· The inability of the Communists to "arouse the masses" in conjunction with last year's Tet offensive was a conclusive demonstration that in the active military theater—in South Vietnam itself—the Communists have failed to achieve or even approximate either their military or their political goals.

· Numerous indirect consequences of the American military intervention have also been positive and important. It is certain . . . that Indonesia would have succumbed to its Communists instead of smashing them if it had not been for the fact that the Americans were holding firm in Vietnam. American military firmness has been an essential condition, also, for the relatively favorable political climate throughout the region.

*   *   *   *   *

· Whatever may be the merits of the original decision to intervene massively in Vietnam, the *fact* of the intervention, continued several years, creates an unavoidable commitment. This commitment is three-fold:

· to the people of South Vietnam, who must face the consequences of the war against the Communists, whatever the Americans do in the future;

· to the American people, who have had to furnish lives and money for the war, and to suffer its domestic consequences;

· to other nations, and to world opinion—whatever their views on the war's justification—that will judge the credibility of the United States by its success or failure in achieving the minimum objective, and will draw the consequences of this judgment in practice.

What Do You Think?

1.   . . . "the nature of the communist aggression in Vietnam . . . made intervention politically compelling. Failure to intervene in South Vietnam would only have postponed the decision a few years until the identical issue would have been posed in relation to mounting attacks in Thailand, Malaysia, or India . . ." What evidence exists to support or refute this viewpoint?

2.   Should the nations of the world expect American troops to help them when they face a communist military threat? Explain your reasoning.

3.   Accept for the sake of argument that the war in Vietnam is one phase of a communist program to take over the world.

What ways other than war might there be to stop the communists? Give reasons for your answer.

Senators Speak on Vietnam *

The United States Senate has often acted as a watchdog on foreign policy—by exercising its power to advise and consent on treaties and appointment of ambassadors and cabinet members, and through its legislative role in determining military appropriations and the maximum size of the military. Senate sentiment on such issues as American policy on Vietnam is of the utmost importance. Here are the views of some Senators about Vietnam in 1965.

Georgia Democrat Richard Russell, chairman of the Armed Services Committee: "The West has made about every conceivable blunder in Viet Nam since the time the fighting started over there. But there isn't a way out just now. We are deeply committed, and it's been a growing commitment."

Mississippi Democrat John Stennis, chairman of the Senate Preparedness Subcommittee: "Within the Senate, there is solid support for standing firm in Viet Nam. Within the group, there are a great many regrets that we are in there. But we are in there. Our flag is committed. Our boys are committed. We've got to back them up. We would invite much more serious trouble elsewhere in Asia and throughout the world if we set a precedent in being pushed out. I regret that we got in there. And I regret the extent to which we have become committed—particularly because we are committed alone. I don't think we can continue to go it alone indefinitely. I continue to think that others will help us in Viet Nam. We can't pull out."

South Carolina Republican Strom Thurmond: "If we are going to follow a non-win policy, as we have in practically all of our conflicts with the Communists since World War II, then we might as well get out now, rather than be negotiated out later, resulting in eventual surrender and the loss of many young American lives. I still believe, as did General MacArthur, that there is no substitute for victory."

Florida Democrat George Smathers: "We're not looking for any glory out there. It's not a question of how we got there or why. We're there. The question is, what do we do?"

Oklahoma Democrat Fred Harris: "We can't predict that we will have the right results in Viet Nam, but our actions are rightly conceived. I

* Excerpted from "The Senate On Viet Nam: Anxiety & Assent," *Time,* August 13, 1965. © 1965 Time, Inc.

know this is the only course we can follow. Nobody is really happy about it. Events are controlling us, and no one likes to be controlled by events. Within the limits of his options, President Johnson is doing his best to control events. There isn't anything to do but what the President is doing. . . .

"Where does it end? We don't know. That's disturbing and somewhat distressing."

Maine Democrat Edmund Muskie: "I don't have any alternatives that I consider realistic or any more effective than what the President is using. Trying to play the game looking over his shoulder without seeing his cards is difficult to do. On the face of it, I can't accept the idea of withdrawal. I feel unhappy about Viet Nam—but I'm not particularly rebellious. The idea of the measured response is what bothers people. They'd like a more clear-cut way to reach objectives. I don't see how he could go further on the peace offensive than he has without some indication that the enemy is receptive."

Wyoming Democrat Gale McGee: "In Viet Nam today, we are experiencing a clandestine form of international Communist aggression which stands as the greatest remaining threat to peace in the world. This insidious aggression, known as 'wars of national liberation,' stands on trial in Viet Nam. If it succeeds, it can only lead to further aggression elsewhere. But if it fails, we can hope that aggression may be over forever."

What Do You Think?

1. Under what conditions (if any) would you advocate sending American troops to another country?
2. Which Senator's viewpoint makes the most sense to you? The least? Why?

Teen-agers Speak *

Youth around the world have shown a strong interest in the Vietnam War. Senior Scholastic *magazine asked a panel of youth from various countries to discuss youth's opinions of our presence in Vietnam and of our attitudes toward communism. How do the views of these young people compare with yours?*

---

* Excerpted from "Old Values and New Realities," *Senior Scholastic,* April 25, 1968. By permission *Senior Scholastic.* © 1968 Scholastic Magazines, Inc.

Claus (Brazil): Throughout history, war was considered a solution to problems. It can no longer be so.

Moderator: One of the foreign students here is from a country whose present reality *is* war. What's your answer, Diep, to the charge that war is unrealistic? What do you believe the South Vietnamese are fighting for?

Diep Chu (South Viet Nam): We are fighting for freedom.

Moderator: How would you define that? Freedom for what or from what?

Diep Chu (South Viet Nam): From the Communists.

Audrey Turner (Louisiana): We were discussing this among ourselves last night, and we came to the conclusion that if communism works better for a country, and its people think it would do better as a Communist country, then they should have the right to be Communist. But if we feel that democracy works better for our country, then we should keep our system. If each country could determine its own system freely, without outside intervention, then this would be a much more peaceful place.

Moderator: But what happens when you live in a country such as India and the Red Chinese announce that they want part of India and they start sending troops across the border? It's no longer a case of the people having a say. What then?

Indira Viswanathan (India): When it comes to Red China, it's not just a question of we in India not wanting communism, but of the Chinese wanting our land. It's a question of national identity, not ideology.

Bill Campbell (California): One myth that I'd like to point out is that a lot of people still consider communism an absolute evil, and any negotiation and compromise with communism is therefore tyranny. This simply does not fit the realistic situation today. It has been shown that systems of government evolve to meet man's basic needs. You can see that the U.S. is gradually evolving towards a form of socialism while the Soviet Union is gradually accepting more capitalism.

*   *   *   *   *

Tomie McCall (Arkansas): I'd like to ask Diep this question. Would the average Vietnamese person know enough about democratic government versus a Communist government to choose wisely if there were to be an election?

Diep Chu (South Viet Nam): Most of the South Vietnamese are rice farmers and do not really know much about governments. Most of them want a comfortable life and a chance for education.

Philip Hebbelthwaite (Australia): I'm probably taking a very cold look at it, but you have this Communist advance in Southeast Asia and it has got to be stopped somewhere. It is in South Viet Nam at the moment, so why not stop it there?

Nick Nelson (Georgia):   The Communists have said many times what they will do to our way of life. They are trying to do the same thing in South Viet Nam, so we have every right to go in and protect the South Vietnamese. If somebody steps on my foot, I have a right to protect myself to see that they don't step on my foot again.

What Do You Think?

1. "One myth . . . is that a lot of people still consider communism an absolute evil, and any negotiation and compromise with communism is therefore tyranny." How would you react to this statement? Why?

2. Which do you think is more important in a situation such as the Vietnam War: that there be peace, or that the people involved may have the type of government they wish, be it democracy or communism? Are there other alternatives?

2.   SHOULD THE UNITED STATES HAVE INTERVENED? NO!

In the preceding section you read that the United States entered Vietnam to contain communism and to safeguard freedom and democracy. Yet, many learned people think America's approach to the Vietnam problem is not achieving what is intended.

We Are Deluding Ourselves in Vietnam *

Hans Morgenthau, a noted political scientist, offers the following argument against our policy:

We are militarily engaged in Viet-Nam by virtue of a basic principle of our foreign policy that was implicit in the Truman Doctrine of 1947 and was put into practice by Secretary of State John Foster Dulles from 1954 onward. This principle is the military containment of communism. Containment had its origins in Europe; Dulles applied it to the Middle East and Asia through a series of bilateral and multilateral alliances. Yet what was an outstanding success in Europe turned out to be a dismal failure elsewhere. The reasons for that failure are twofold.

First, the threat that faced the nations of Western Europe in the aftermath of the Second World War was primarily military. It was the

---

* Excerpted from Hans Morgenthau. "We Are Deluding Ourselves in Vietnam," *The New York Times Magazine*, April 18, 1965. © 1965 by The New York Times Company. Reprinted by permission.

threat of the Red Army marching westward. Behind the line of military demarcation of 1945, which the policy of containment declared to be the western-most limit of the Soviet empire, there was an ancient civilization, only temporarily weak and able to maintain itself against the threat of Communist subversion.

The situation is different in the Middle East and Asia. The threat there is not primarily military but political in nature. Weak governments and societies provide opportunities for Communist subversion. Military containment is irrelevant to that threat. . . .

Second, and more important, even if China were threatening her neighbors primarily by military means, it would be impossible to contain her by erecting a military wall at the periphery of her empire. For China is, even in her present underdeveloped state, the dominant power in Asia. She is this by virtue of the quality and quantity of her population, her geographic position, her civilization, her past power remembered and her future power anticipated. Anybody who has traveled in Asia with his eyes and ears open must have been impressed by the enormous impact which the resurgence of China has made upon all manner of men, regardless of class and political conviction, from Japan to Pakistan.

The issue China poses is political and cultural predominance. The United States can no more contain Chinese influence in Asia by arming South Vietnam and Thailand than China could contain American influence in the Western Hemisphere by arming, say Nicaragua and Costa Rica.

*   *   *   *   *

[W]e must learn to accommodate ourselves to the predominance of China on the Asian mainland. It is instructive to note that those Asian nations which have done so—such as Burma and Cambodia—live peacefully in the shadow of the Chinese giant.

What Do You Think?

Morgenthau states: "We must learn to accommodate ourselves to the predominance of China on the Asian mainland." How might Robert McNamara respond to this statement? How would you respond?

Dangers Lurk for the United States *

Many journalists have been critical of America's participation in Vietnam. Marcus Raskins is a journalist who not only has written against this participation but has also spoken against it at public meet-

---

* Excerpted from the *Congressional Record,* May 5, 1965.

ings and demonstrations. What dangers does he see for the United States in Vietnam?

Since the Second World War, American policymakers have developed a foreign policy that casts America in the role of world policeman. We assumed this role in Viet-Nam, a place where we did not begin to comprehend the complex crosscurrents of politics, nationalism, personality, tradition, history, and other people's interests. To support our role as policeman, our military and C.I.A. programs in Southeast Asia grew to mammoth proportions without rhyme or reason. These programs often reflected little more than the power struggles of the agencies of American bureaucracy, rather than the reality of the Asian situation. A report on Viet-Nam and Southeast Asia prepared in 1963 by four Senators, at the request of President Kennedy, stated:

It should also be noted, in all frankness, that our own bureaucratic tendencies to act in uniform and enlarging patterns have resulted in an expansion of the U.S. commitment in some places to an extent which would appear to bear only the remotest relationship to what is essential, or even desirable, in terms of U.S. interests.

The United States, by the military and covert way it has operated in Viet-Nam in the past ten years, has nurtured strong anti-white and anti-Western feelings in Southeast Asia. Whether we called it "responsibility" or empire, the fact is that the United States succeeded to the Japanese and French hegemony in Asia without really knowing why or with what purpose. Empires are very seldom built by design. They start almost accidentally: their dynamics and actions define what they are. Each empire has its own characteristics, although historically they all seem to involve the defense of allies, the suppression of certain regimes in favor of others, and a powerful ideology. Ultimately, a common characteristic is a lack of judgment on the part of leaders, who are no longer able to distinguish between real and chimeric [1] interests because of the empire's octopus-like tentacles. Those tentacles, especially if they include extensive military involvement, strangle the judgment of the leaders.

Our military involvement in Viet-Nam has camouflaged America's real interests and distorted our diplomatic and political vision of the means that should be employed there. The methods we have followed in Viet-Nam may not be without cost in terms of our own nation's stability and freedom of choice. Thus, when we ask the military to undertake projects which are inherently unmilitary, we are courting great danger. . . . For example, the official American policy in South Viet-Nam is to support a civilian government, but the rank-and-file military as well as high-ranking Amer-

---

[1] illusory

ican military officers in Viet-Nam support the South Vietnamese military. Bad habits are learned in such wars and they may too easily be applied at home.

It is hard for American civilian leadership to learn that the military is not a machine which can be started and stopped by pressing a button. By definition of their mission, the military want to follow through to a military victory. We will find that each day that American policy-makers procrastinate on a political settlement, the war will escalate just by its own momentum. In this regard the military bureaucratic course of the war is quite instructive. The Special Forces and the Army were given responsibility for the war, under President Kennedy. After the apparent failure of these forces, the Air Force lobbied for involvement. Using the Gulf of Tonkin as the pretext, the Air Force sent planes to South Viet-Nam as a "deterrent." But "deterrents" are vulnerable and can be easily destroyed by guerrillas, as these were at Bien Hoa. Here the psychology of the paper tiger played its part. The pride of the Air Force was wounded and it decided to involve itself more fully so that it could prove itself. Once this occurred, the Marines and the Navy . . . lobbied for an expanded role, which was granted. Not wanting to be left out, the Army also petitioned for greater involvement. This was also granted by the White House. Finally, the S.A.C.,[2] in a non-nuclear way, also wanted to be involved. Paradoxically, the military may have wished for involvement because they feared that the war would end, that the "politicians" would negotiate a military withdrawal before they had had a chance to test themselves in battle. While our military may have feared that the war would be over, it was very hard to impress on our opponents our peaceful intentions, or to counter those groups in the American government and the public who wanted a military "win."

As a military venture, the Vietnamese operation is not one in which very many can take any particular pride. The bad habits of that war have included torture, napalming, and defoliation, as well as an inability to understand which means could yield suitable ends. . . . Too often . . . men in government . . . are expected to operate under inverted definitions of responsibility and morality, or to forget about them while in government. . . . This sort of "responsibility" and "morality" can be seen in Viet-Nam. Where, as in the case of Viet-Nam, three out of four Americans were not even aware until the middle of 1964 that the United States was involved militarily, officials seem to have felt themselves free to tolerate sadistic and totalitarian methods in the name of fuzzy objectives. Such methods spread easily, and unthinkingly, in governments. It is best that they be exposed and terminated.

---

[2] Strategic Air Command

What Do You Think?

What role do you think the military should play in the formulation of America's foreign policy?

What War Means to the Vietnamese People *

Senator Robert Kennedy was concerned about the effects of warfare on the Vietnamese people. Ending the war was one of the major points upon which he based his campaign for the Democratic Party's presidential nomination in 1968. During the campaign, a book of his views on important issues was published. This statement on Vietnam is from that book. What did Kennedy see happening to the Vietnamese people? Do the effects of war clearly indicate that the war must stop?

VIETNAM. The astounding might of American power now falls upon a remote and alien people in a small and unknown land. It is difficult to feel in our hearts what this war means to Vietnam; it is on the other side of the world, and its people are strangers. Few of us are directly involved, while the rest of us continue our lives and pursue our ambitions undisturbed by the sounds and fears of battle. To the Vietnamese, however, it must often seem the fulfillment of the prophecy of Saint John the Divine: "And I looked, and beheld a pale horse: and his name that sat on him was Death, and Hell followed with him. And power was given unto them over the fourth part of the earth, to kill with sword, with hunger, and with death. . . ."

Although the world's imperfections may call forth the acts of war, righteousness cannot obscure the agony and pain those acts bring to a single child. The Vietnamese war is an event of historic moment, summoning the power and concern of many nations. But it is also the vacant moment of amazed fear as a mother and child watch death by fire fall from the improbable machine sent by a country they barely comprehend. It is the sudden terror of the official or the hamlet militiaman absorbed in the work of his village as he realizes the assassin is taking his life. It is the refugees wandering homeless from villages now obliterated, leaving behind only those who did not live to flee. It is the young men, Vietnamese and American, who in an instant sense the night of death destroying yesterday's promise of family and land and home.

It is a country where young men have never lived a day in peace and where families have never known a time when it was not necessary to be

* From *To Seek a Newer World* by Robert F. Kennedy. Copyright © 1967 Robert F. Kennedy. Reprinted by permission of Doubleday & Company, Inc.

afraid. It is a land deafened by the unending crescendo of violence, hatred, and savage fury, where the absorbing goal for millions is not to live well or to improve their lives, but simply to survive. It is a country where hundreds of thousands fight, but millions more are the innocent, bewildered victims of brutal passions and beliefs they barely understand. To them peace is not an abstract term describing one of those infrequent intervals when men are not killing each other. It is a day without terror and the fall of bombs. It is a family and the familiar life of their village. It is food and a school and life itself.

All we say and all we do must be informed by our awareness that this horror is partly our responsibility; not just a nation's responsibility but yours and mine. It is we who live in abundance and send our young men out to die. It is our chemicals that scorch the children and our bombs that level the villages. We are all participants. To know this, to feel the burden of this responsibility, is not to ignore important interests, nor to forget that freedom and security must sometimes be paid for in blood. Still even though we must know as a nation what it is necessary to do, we must also feel as men the anguish of what it is we are doing.

What Do You Think?

1. How do Senator Kennedy's feelings on the Vietnam war differ from the others given in this chapter?
2. "Still even though we must know as a nation what is necessary to do, we must also feel as men the anguish of what it is we are doing." What do you think Senator Kennedy means by this?
3. "What has happened to the Vietnamese people is the price they must accept for the war Americans are fighting for them to keep them free from communist domination." How might a Vietnamese react to this statement?

ACTIVITIES FOR INVOLVEMENT

1. Write a letter to the *National Review,* in which you explain why you agree or disagree with its viewpoint.

2. Choose the viewpoint of one of the Senators in this Chapter. Write that Senator a letter, responding to what he said.

3. After doing further research on the views of Hans Morgenthau and Robert McNamara, hold a round-table discussion in which various members of the class present a summary of what they have found and then discuss how they think each man would respond to the others' arguments.

4. Hold a panel discussion on the topic: "Resolved: That the United States should never have become involved in Vietnam."

5.   Have two students enact the following sociodrama: A Vietnamese peasant comes to an American military headquarters to ask the commanding officer not to attack his village. The commanding officer engages in dialogue with another officer who has just received information that enemy troops are hiding in the village.

6.   Hold a panel discussion in which several class members present as much evidence as they can find on the views of General Thomas Powers, Senator Robert Kennedy, Marcus Raskins, and Senator Strom Thurmond as to the role of American troops in Vietnam.

7.   Form a small committee to research the incident at My Lai in South Vietnam in March of 1968. After the committee has reported its findings, hold a mock "Meet the Press" program in which two members of the class attempt to explain the Army's actions in this situation, and the balance of the class portrays inquiring reporters who question the Army's position.

Political Involvement

4

In April, 1961, 1500 Cubans invaded their homeland to overthrow Fidel Castro's regime. They were trained and equipped in Guatemala and Florida by the United States Central Intelligence Agency. As you read, ask yourself: What do you think of the United States' participating in such a scheme? Should a nation engage in trying to get rid of governments it doesn't like or considers dangerous to its own existence? Keep these questions in mind as you read of a similar action in the Dominican Republic in 1965.

1. THE C. I. A. ATTEMPTS TO OVERTHROW CASTRO *

The following is one account of United States involvement in the Bay of Pigs invasion.

ARTIME'S STORY

The counter-revolution had not begun suddenly or dramatically. No martyrs vainly charged fortress walls or declared to their judges, as Fidel himself had done, that "History will absolve me!" No heroic symbols, figures or dates foreshadowed in Fidel's first year, of 1959, after he entered Havana in triumph.

Through all the events that year, the broken pledges of free elections and a free press, the mass trials and executions, the arrogant assumption of unlimited power and the bellicose threats against the United States, Fidel remained the unchallenged leader. It was his revolution. To the masses, as well as to many in the professions, he was still *El Caballo* (The Horse),

---

* Excerpted from Haynes Johnson. *The Bay of Pigs: The Leaders' Story of Brigade 2506.* By permission of W. W. Norton & Company, Inc. Copyright © 1964 by Haynes Johnson.

the romantic, quixotic, legendary liberator from the hills. And yet as the Cuban revolution—the genuine political, economic and social revolution that Fidel had promised and the people had prayed for—turned into another form of dictatorship, a sense of betrayal began to grow.

Probably the first clear sign occurred on October 19, 1959, when Major Huber Matos, one of the highest-ranking officers in Fidel's rebel forces, resigned from the army in protest against the increasing favoritism shown to known Communists. The next day Matos was arrested at his home, charged with treason, and subsequently tried and sentenced to twenty years in prison. A few days after his arrest, a secret meeting of the National Agrarian Reform Institute (INRA) managers of Cuba was held in Havana. There, the suspicions of Dr. Manuel Francisco Artime, the young manager in Oriente Province, were confirmed. He heard Fidel personally outline a plan to communize Cuba within three years.

"I realized," Artime said, "that I was a democratic infiltrator in a Communist government."

Artime returned to Oriente, took a leave of absence, and with a group of college students began preparing the peasants to fight against Castro and communism. Many still had arms left over from the battle against Batista,[1] and once more they stored them in the Sierra Maestra Mountains. By early November the basis for an underground movement in each province had been formed. It was named the *Movimiento de Recuperación Revolucionaria* (MRR) and it was the first action group originating from within Fidel's own ranks. When Fidel's G-2 began searching for the leaders, Artime took asylum with the Jesuits in Havana.

On November 7 Artime's letter of resignation from the rebel army and from the INRA was published on the front page of *Avance* in Havana. Addressed personally to Castro, the letter explained why Artime was resigning "my position in this Red army," referred to the "Red masquerade," and told how he "had heard from your (Castro's) lips the complete plans to communize Cuba." The letter was the sensation of the day. After it appeared a Jesuit priest said he would put Artime in touch with an American who could get him out of the country. Dressed as a priest and carrying a pistol hidden inside a missal, Artime walked up the steps to the American Embassy and met an American, a man he knew as "Williams."

While the American hid Artime in his own apartment, he asked many questions about Castro and Communist infiltrators. The information, "Williams" said, was being passed on to the United States; he thought the government would be interested in talking to Artime. . . .

It is not clear whether or not the United States Central Intelligence Agency had decided that Castro was a Communist and must be forcibly

---

[1] Fulgencio Batista, dictator deposed by Castro

overthrown by the time CIA agents spirited Artime out of Cuba. As late as November 5, 1959, General Charles P. Cabell, the deputy director of the CIA, testifying behind the closed doors of the Senate Internal Security Sub-committee, said that "we believe that Castro is not a member of the Communist Party, and does not consider himself to be a Communist." General Cabell did say, however, that Castro already had delegated power to persons believed to be Communist sympathizers. . . .

Whether the United States could have done anything short of force, to alter the course of Castro's revolution is an unanswerable question. What is important is that a void in policy did exist. In time that vacuum was filled principally by the CIA, which for its own sources and purposes turned first to Manuel Artime.

Artime's escape from Cuba followed what came to be the standard CIA procedure. When the freighter carrying him from Cuba docked in the bright morning sunshine at Tampa, Florida, Artime was met on the pier by a tall, white-haired American with glasses who introduced himself as "Mr. Burnett, a friend of Williams." There on the dock Artime heard for the first time the story that would be repeated again and again: Burnett did not work for the United States government, but he was employed by a large group of wealthy capitalists who were fighting communism and who had influential friends in the government and in Washington.

Artime and Burnett left for Miami, and from that time on the young Cuban doctor was in the hands of the CIA.

*　　*　　*　　*　　*

On March 17, 1960, President Eisenhower authorized the CIA to organize, train and equip Cuban refugees as a guerrilla force to overthrow Castro. Six years before, the President had made a similar decision involving the CIA, "guerrillas," and a Latin Country—Guatemala. That time it had worked, and the pro-Communist government of Jacobo Arbenz was overthrown by Castillo Armas, a man hand-picked by the CIA. The CIA and the administration clearly hoped for the same success in Cuba.

Artime, through the help of the CIA, had been on a speaking tour of Central and Latin America attempting to rally support for action against Castro. As he traveled through Costa Rica, Panama, Venezuela, Peru and Chile, he received calls from a "Jaime Castillo." In each country "Jaime" had a different voice, but always asked if there were anything he could do to help Artime. In Rio de Janeiro, at the end of March, "Jaime" called again. This time he wanted to see Artime urgently; he was in the hotel lobby and asked to come up immediately. "Jaime" turned out to be an American who spoke Spanish fluently. He insisted that Artime fly immediately to New York to meet some "friends" who wanted to talk to him. It was, he said, vital to the future of Cuba.

"He told me that as soon as I arrived in New York, I should go to the Statler Hilton and say I was George L. Ringo and that I have a room at the hotel," Artime said.

And so Artime flew to New York and checked in at the hotel. He had been in his room only a few minutes when the phone rang.

"Mr. Ringo?"

"Yes, I am Mr. Ringo."

But the caller was speaking in English and Artime could not understand him well. The caller hung up, and the phone rang again.

"Mr. Ringo."

This was a voice Artime understood and recognized. It was Oscar Echevarria, a friend from Cuba who had studied with Artime in college. Echevarria and another Cuban whom Artime knew and trusted, Angel Fernandez Varela, came to the room. They explained that some prominent Cubans who had opposed Batista wanted to contact Artime to see if he would join them in a common cause against Castro. One of the men, Justo Carrillo, already had fled to the United States. The others, Manuel Antonio de Varone, a former Prime Minister of Cuba and president of the Senate; José Ignacio Rasco, a university professor and leader of the new Christian Democratic Party; and Aureliano Sánchez Arango, who had been Minister of Education and Minister of Foreign Relations, were still in Cuba. (Within two months these men and Artime formed their *Frente,* or united exile front, to overthrow Fidel.)

Artime said he opened his arms to them; then he asked what the Americans had to do with this. His friends told him an important American wanted to meet him now and explain that himself. They parted with an *abrazo,* or embrace, and Artime waited. There was a knock on the door and when Artime opened it he saw a tall man, expensively dressed, accompanied by one of his Cuban friends The American introduced himself.

"It was the first time I heard his name," Artime said later, "I was going to hear that name until the Bay of Pigs. Frank Bender. The Great Frank Bender. 'All right, Manolo,' Bender said, 'we've got lots to talk about. I am the man in charge of the Cuban case.' "

Bender repeated the explanation that Artime had heard so often: the great company of wealthy people he represented had directed a large part of its money and effort toward the solution of the Cuban problem, and the defeat of communism everywhere. They had nothing to do with the American government, Bender told him, but they did have influence. Then he asked for Artime's thoughts on the future of Cuba.

"I told him that Cuba could not return to the old corrupt government," Artime said, "that a return to a military dictatorship would lead once more down the road to communism. I told him I believed we needed a genuinely democratic government. We needed social justice. We had to fight unemployment and raise the standard of living of the workers; we had to establish cooperatives to protect the small farmer and the small land owner; and we had to enact social laws to protect old people; we needed a progressive income tax, as in the United States. I told him that if we didn't do these things, we would go back to a corrupt democracy and then again we would have a military dictator who would destroy democracy. And, in the end, a reaction that would lead again to communism. I also told him that I thought the propaganda being used against Castro was wrong. When I went to South America, the people were being warned against Castro because he had taken the land of the rich people. The poor Indians said 'good' and applauded."

Bender apparently was impressed. He listened quietly as Artime discussed his ideas for a guerrilla uprising in Oriente Province, and then Bender asked, "Why not an uprising all over the island?" Artime said he didn't have enough men or weapons for that.

"Well, Artime, what if I told you that we have men who will help you to prepare for guerrilla warfare and others who will prepare men to fight in a conventional war with army training?"

"And you will give us the weapons?"

"All the weapons you need," Bender replied. "And also we will train radio operators so you can be in contact directly with Cuba."

Bender wanted to know if Artime could get men out of Cuba to be trained for such an operation. Artime replied that he could.

"Fine," Bender said, as he got up and handed Artime a piece of paper. "Call this number whenever you need me. Just say 'To Frank Bender from Manolo' and I will come to the phone." He instructed Artime to go to Miami where more friends would be in touch with him, and said he had reserved a plane ticket for him; Artime could pick it up at the hotel. "When you leave," the American said, "don't bother about paying the hotel bill. Just throw the key on the desk in the lobby."

As he left the room, Bender shook hands and said, "Remember, Manolo, I am not a member of the United States government. I am only working for a powerful company that wants to fight communism."

What Do You Think?

1. Why did Bender and Burnett repeatedly insist they were not working for the United States Government?

2. Is it proper for the United States to support nationalist groups to overthrow their governments? Does it make a difference if the governments are Communist or non-Communist? Does it make a difference if the governments are democratic or dictatorial? Explain your reasoning.

3. Should President Eisenhower have consulted congressional

leaders before authorizing the C.I.A. to assist the anti-Castro
forces? Why, or why not?

4.   Is it more acceptable for a dictatorship, such as Russia, than
     a democracy, such as the United States, to operate an agency
     like the C.I.A.? Explain.

5.   Should the United States admit it was behind the invasion to
     get rid of Castro? What if the invasion had succeeded?

6.   How might the perception of an individual like this affect his
     decisions?

2.   SHOULD THE UNITED STATES HAVE BECOME INVOLVED? YES!

*The anti-Castro invasion of Cuba ended in failure only a few days
after it began. Most of the invaders, about 1500 men, were captured
and imprisoned for twenty months. The United States was embarrassed
for supporting this ill-fated venture in attempting to overthrow another
country's government. By December, 1962, several hundred of the
invaders of the 2506th Brigade had been ransomed and brought to
Florida. There, at the Orange Bowl, a large stadium, President Kennedy was given the brigade's flag, as a symbol of solidarity between
the counter-revolutionaries and the United States. Why had the United
States supported the brigade? Although the decision to aid the anti-
Castro invaders had been made by President Eisenhower's Administration, the invasion took place during the Kennedy Administration.
Therefore, it was left to President Kennedy to explain why America
had supported the invaders.*

President Kennedy Praises Brigade 2506 As Heroic Historical Figures *

All of you members of the brigade . . . are following an historic road,
one which has been followed by other Cubans in other days, and indeed,
by other patriots of our hemisphere in other years . . . All of whom
fought for liberty, many of whom were defeated, many of whom went into
exile, and all of whom came home.

Seventy years ago José Marti, the guiding spirit of the first Cuban
struggle for independence, lived on these shores. At that time in 1889 the
first international American conference was held, and Cuba was not present. Then, as now, Cuba was the only state in the hemisphere still controlled by a foreign monarch. Then, as now, Cuba was excluded from the

---

* Excerpted from "President Kennedy Accepts Custody of the Flag of Cuban
Brigade 2506," *United States State Department Bulletin,* XLVIII, December 29,
1962.

society of free nations. And then, as now, brave men in Florida and New York dedicated their lives and their energies to the freedom of their homeland.

The brigade comes from behind prison walls, but you leave behind you more than 6 million of your fellow countrymen who are also in a very real sense in prison, for Cuba is today, as Marti described it many years ago . . .—a prison moated by water.

On behalf of my Government and my country, I welcome you to the United States. I bring you my nation's respect for your courage and for your cause. . . .

[Y]our small brigade is a tangible reaffirmation that the human desire for freedom and independence is essentially unconquerable. Your conduct and valor are proof that, although Castro and his fellow dictators may rule nations, they do not rule people; that they may imprison bodies, but they do not imprison spirits; that they may destroy the exercise of liberty, but they cannot eliminate the determination to be free. And by helping to free you the United States has been given the opportunity to demonstrate once again that all men who fight for freedom are our brothers and shall be until your country and others are free.

The Cuban people were promised by the revolution political liberty, social justice, intellectual freedom, land for the *compesinos,* and an end to economic exploitation. They have received a police state, the elimination of the dignity of land ownership, the destruction of free speech and of free press, and the complete subjugation of individual human welfare to the service of the state and of foreign states.

*   *   *   *   *

The brigade is the point of the spear, the arrow's head. I hope they and the members of their families will take every opportunity to educate your children, yourselves, in the many skills and disciplines which will be necessary when Cuba is once more free.

Finally, I can offer no better advice than that given by José Marti to his fellow exiles in 1895, when the hour of Cuban independence was then at hand. "Let the tenor of our words be," Marti said, "especially in public matters, not the useless clamor of fear's vengeance which does not enter our hearts, but the honest weariness of an oppressed people who hope through their emancipation from a government convicted of uselessness and malevolence, for a government of their own which is capable and worthy . . ."

What Do You Think?

1. Supporting an effort by rebels to overthrow another country's government is a serious international affair. President Kennedy

suggests there is also another issue involved. What is it? Would
you agree? Explain.

2.   Why did the United States support the Bay of Pigs invasion?

3. SHOULD THE UNITED STATES HAVE BECOME INVOLVED? NO!

To some people, American participation in an effort to overthrow an-
other government was a violation of America's professed support of
the principle of self-determination of nations. Others were angry be-
cause the United States had bungled the job. Americans have been
critical of Russia's use of military force to overthrow the governments
of Hungary in 1956 and Czechoslovakia in 1968. Is there a difference,
when we support armed force against a government we don't like?

The Bay of Pigs Fiasco: Criticism from the Public *

Post-mortems are often painful, but they are necessary in military and
political affairs and they can be salutary. No one can have any doubt today
that there has been a great deal of miscalculation, misunderstanding,
wishful thinking and underestimation of the factors involved inside and
outside of Cuba.

It is now common knowledge that the United States played a con-
siderable role in the preparations for the episode and that specifically the
Central Intelligence Agency masterminded the operation for the American
Government, first during the Eisenhower Administration and then under
President Kennedy.

*   *   *   *   *

[A]s is now clear, basic and inexcusable miscalculations were made
by the C.I.A. The latter was badly and inadequately informed about the
situation in Cuba from the beginning, perhaps with some unconscious pre-
conceptions, and consequently it underestimated the magnitude of the
problems and presumably gave poor advice to the White House and the
State Department. It contributed to the division among the exiles by backing the Democratic Revolutionary Front almost exclusively and shoulder-
ing aside the M.R.P. (Revolutionary Movement of the People), which had
the best underground organization in Cuba.

The responsibility, under our system of government, is the President's,
and he is accepting it. The obvious consequences of this setback are a
strengthening of the Castro regime, a weakening of the Cuban exiles, a

---

* Excerpted from *The New York Times,* April 22, 1961. © 1961 by The New
York Times Company. Reprinted by permission.

considerable propaganda victory for the Soviet bloc and a loss of prestige by the United States. . . .

The harsh lessons of the week must not be ignored. A great power must take setbacks as well as victories. This has been a setback, but it is not the end.

Letters to the Editor *

An Open Telegram to President Kennedy:

U. S. Government engaged in incredible breach of peace at attack on Cuba. No one in Latin America, I repeat, no one will believe U. S. was not organizer of it. You are playing with lives, not of thousands, but of billions.

*   *   *   *   *

While aware of the many problems Castro has posed for the United States, I think we should not forget previous statements this country has made concerning self-determination of countries, including those bordering on the U.S.S.R. Do we adhere to our principles only when it is convenient?

"An Appeal to Americans . . ." *

[Secretary of State] . . . Rusk has presumed to speak for the American people. He announced this week that "it is no secret that the American people's sympathy is with those fighting against the dictatorship" of Fidel Castro.

It must come as news to everyone that the American people have ever been consulted in this matter. We believe that Mr. Rusk speaks not for the American people but for the Central Intelligence Agency and the State Department. Certainly he does not speak for us.

We believe that no government has the right to overthrow any other government whose domestic and foreign policies do not meet its approval.

.   We believe that by financing, arming and training Cuban counter-revolutionaries, we have violated not only our own laws but our treaty obligations as well. As a member of the Organization of American States, and as a member of the United Nations, we are bound to respect the recognized governments of other countries, whether we like them or not.

If, as our government declares, we are opposed to "dictatorship"; and if, in fact, that is our reason for intervening in Cuba's domestic affairs, may we expect that in the near future our government will aid other exiles?

---

* Excerpted from *The San Francisco Chronicle,* April 24, 1961 and April 26, 1961, editorial pages.
* Excerpted from *The New York Times,* April 21, 1961. Advertisement of the Fair Play for Cuba Committee.

Are we going to arm, train, and finance the Portuguese and Spanish exiles who want to overthrow the dictatorships, in those countries? *We believe that the Cuban people have the right to determine their own destiny, their own foreign and domestic policies, without intervention from the United States Government.*

What Do You Think?

1. Some people have said that the only valid criticism of the C.I.A.-supported invasion of Castro's Cuba is that it failed and thus damaged the United States' image. Would you agree? Why or why not?

2. The Fair Play for Cuba Committee stated in *The New York Times* advertisement of April 21, 1961: "We believe that by financing, arming and training Cuban counterrevolutionaries, we have violated not only our own laws but our treaty obligations as well." Would you agree? Explain. If Castro's Cuba was participating in a program to harm the United States, would you change your position in any way? Why or why not?

3. The Fair Play for Cuba Committee also stated: "No government has the right to overthrow any other government whose domestic and foreign policies do not meet its approval." What arguments might someone use to support or refute this view?

4. AMERICAN TROOPS IN THE DOMINICAN REPUBLIC

The intervention into the Dominican Republic in 1965 was extensively, and in some cases bitterly, opposed in the United States. To many it smacked of the old and rejected Big Stick tactics of Theodore Roosevelt. Criticism came from many quarters, including J. William Fulbright, chairman of the powerful Senate Foreign Relations Committee, and such newspapers as The New York Times *and the* San Francisco Chronicle. *Others felt it was a necessary action to protect United States interests. The following readings offer varying shades of opinion about what our role has been or should be in Latin America and elsewhere. Are we guardians of freedom or meddlers in the internal affairs of others? Are there other ways to accomplish our goals?*

Senator Fulbright Denounces the "Arrogance of Power" *

Nowhere has the ambivalence [1] in the American attitude toward revolu-

---

* Excerpted from J. William Fulbright, *The Arrogance of Power*. Copyright 1966 by J. William Fulbright. Reprinted by permission of Random House, Inc.
[1] simultaneous attraction toward and repulsion against

tion been more apparent and more troublesome than in the relations of the United States with Latin America. In Latin America as in Asia the United States, a profoundly unrevolutionary nation, is required to make choices between accepting revolution and trying to suppress it.

*　　*　　*　　*　　*

The election on June 1, 1966, of Joachin Balaguer as President of the Dominican Republic, in an election regarded by most observers as having been fair and free, has been widely interpreted as a vindication of the American military intervention of April 1965, as proof that the intervention was necessary, justified, and wise. Those of us who criticized the American intervention must concede that a degree of order and stability in the Dominican Republic was restored more quickly than seemed likely in the spring and summer of 1965 and that credit for this properly belongs to United States diplomacy, to the Organization of American States, and to the Inter-American Force which remained in the Dominican Republic until the summer of 1966, as well as to the provisional government which held office from September 1965 to July 1966 and to the elected government which succeeded it.

That, however, is all that must or can be conceded. The facts remain that the United States engaged in a unilateral military intervention in violation of inter-American law, the "good neighbor" policy of thirty years standing, and the spirit of the Charter of Punta del Este; that the Organization of American States was gravely weakened as the result of its use—with its own consent—as an instrument of the policy of the United States; that the power of the reactionary military oligarchy in the Dominican Republic remains substantially unimpaired; that the intervention alienated from the United States the confidence and good opinion of reformers and young people throughout Latin America, the very people, that is, whose efforts are essential to the success of peaceful revolution through the Alliance for Progress; and that confidence in the word and in the intentions of the United States Government has been severely shaken, not only in Latin America but in Europe and Asia and even in our own country.

*　　*　　*　　*　　*

The central fact about the intervention of the United States in the Dominican Republic was that we had closed our minds to the causes and to the essential legitimacy of revolution in a country in which democratic procedures had failed. The involvement of an undetermined number of communists in the Dominican Revolution was judged to discredit the entire reformist movement, like poison in a well, and rather than use our considerable resources to compete with the communists for influence with the democratic forces who actively solicited our support, we intervened militarily on the side of a corrupt and reactionary military oligarchy. We thus lent credence to the idea that the United States is the enemy of social revolution, and therefore the enemy of social justice, in Latin America.

*   *   *   *   *

The question of the degree of communist influence is crucial but it cannot be answered with certainty. The weight of the evidence is that communists did not participate in planning the revolution—indeed, there is some indication that it took them by surprise—but that they very rapidly began to try to take advantage of and to seize control of it. The evidence does not establish that the communists at any time actually had control of the revolution. There is little doubt that they had influence within the revolutionary movement, but the degree of that influence remains a matter of speculation.

The United States government, however, assumed almost from the beginning that the revolution was communist-dominated, or would certainly become so, and that nothing short of forcible opposition could prevent a communist takeover. In their panic lest the Dominican Republic become "another Cuba," some of our officials seem to have forgotten that virtually all reform movements attract some communist support, that there is an important difference between communist support and communist control of a political movement, that it is quite possible to compete with the communists for influence in a reform movement rather than abandon it to them, and, most important of all, that economic development and social justice are themselves the primary and most reliable security against communist subversion. The point I am making is not—most emphatically not—that there was no communist participation in the Dominican crisis, but simply that the Administration acted on the premise that the revolution was controlled by communists—a premise which it failed to establish at the time and has not established since.

Intervention on the basis of communist participation as distinguished from control of the Dominican Revolution was a mistake of panic and timidity which also reflects a grievous misreading of the temper of contemporary Latin American politics. Communists are present in all Latin American countries, and they are going to inject themselves into almost any Latin American revolution and try to seize control of it. If any group or any movement with which the communists associate themselves is going to be automatically condemned in the eyes of the United States, then we have indeed given up all hope of influencing even to a marginal degree the revolutionary movements and the demands for social change which are sweeping Latin America. Worse, if that is our view, then we have made ourselves the prisoners of the Latin American oligarchs who are engaged in a vain attempt to preserve the status quo—reactionaries who habitually use the term "communist" very loosely, in part out of emotional predilection and in part in a calculated effort to scare the United States into supporting their selfish and discredited aims.

The movement of the future in Latin America is social revolution. The question is whether it is to be communist or democratic revolution and the choice which the Latin Americans make will depend in part on how the United States uses its great influence. It should be very clear that the choice is not between social revolution and conservative oligarchy but whether, by supporting reform, we bolster the popular non-communist left, or, by supporting unpopular oligarchies, we drive the rising generation of educated and patriotic young Latin Americans to an embittered and hostile form of communism like that of Fidel Castro in Cuba.

Marines in Santo Domingo *

There was a valid reason for the United States to put a Marine landing force into Santo Domingo. This reason was to protect Americans and evacuate those who desire to leave. There would be no excuse for American Marines to remain beyond that short time, unless asked to do so by the *de facto* government. It will be for the Organization of American States to pick up from there.

Only Latin Americans and students of the history of the Caribbean can appreciate fully what it means to have the word flashed around the hemisphere: " 'The American Marines have landed' " The symbol of President Theodore Roosevelt's "Big Stick" and of President Taft's "Dollar Diplomacy" is United States occupation by Marines.

The present move, according to President Johnson, is not intended to be an occupation. He has explained that the troops went ashore "to give protection to hundreds of Americans who are still in the Dominican Republic and to escort them safely back to this country."

This is a right and necessary function; it should be the only one. . . . the O.A.S. has been faced with a *fait accompli* and there appears to be some hard feelings on that score. The United States decision was a unilateral one made, presumably, because there was no Dominican Government empowered to ask for American troops.

*   *   *   *   *

The way things are going to be, the Dominican Republic will need an extended period of peace, one sustained by Dominicans, perhaps with the help of the O.A.S.—but not by American Marines.

---

* Excerpted from *The New York Times,* April 30, 1965. © 1965 by The New York Times Company. Reprinted by permission.

Johnson's Doctrine Applies Monroe's Doctrine to the World *

From the war on poverty to the war in Vietnam, from the Alliance for Progress to the Marines in the Dominican Republic, from common action and collective security to unilateral military force—this has been the melancholy direction of events in the last 120 days.

*   *   *   *   *

At the beginning of the year the President was determined not to go north in Vietnam but went. . . . His formula for unifying the Alliance was common consultation and, if possible, common action, on common problems, but now he is carrying greater burdens with less help from allies than ever.

The Johnson way is changing the use of American power to a significant degree. He is using military power faster now. He is still limiting his retaliatory military moves, but he now seems more ready to go it alone.

*   *   *   *   *

He has gone back to the Monroe Doctrine in dealing with the uprising in the Dominican Republic. The basic principle of the Organization of American States is that "no state or group of states has the right to intervene, directly or indirectly, for any reason whatever, in the internal or external affairs of any other state . . ."

After a year of disappointing efforts to get effective cooperation from the allies, however, the President acted first on reports that he faced another Communist conquest in the Caribbean and consulted later.

Moreover, Mr. Johnson's long comments on the Vietnamese crisis today indicates that the Johnson Doctrine is to apply the Monroe Doctrine not only in this hemisphere but in other parts of the world threatened by Communist power.

What Price Liberalism? *

James Burnham sees President Johnson's motivation for "hard military action" in Santo Domingo as part of a necessary "counter-revolutionary operation in the world struggle against revolutionary Communism." In the following excerpt from his National Review *column "The Third World War," he questions the motivation and judgment of the critics of this policy.*

---

* Excerpted from James Reston, *The New York Times,* May 5, 1965. © 1965 by The New York Times Company. Reprinted by permission.
* Excerpted from James Burnham,"The Third World War, What Price Liberalism?" *National Review,* June 1, 1965.

This country is presently engaged in two very considerable military operations. In Southeast Asia we are in reality at war, and even in the Caribbean we are suffering very real casualties. Meanwhile on the domestic front the opposition to the present course is both widespread and intense.

The President is reported distressed and angry at this opposition to his policy. Well might he be: for it is not merely "his policy" but the nation's security and vital interest that are at stake. They are at stake, or come to be, whether or not the decisions that lead to our involvement were correct. This is the meaning behind the older rule of the loyal citizen: "My country, may she be ever in the right, but my country right or wrong!" Generally speaking, a nation is injured or destroyed by losing a war even if it's the wrong war.

Will the President reflect on the kind of opposition that he has developed, and its primary sources? Hardly any of it comes from the [political] Right. It goes without saying that Communists and other revolutionaries are a part of it, together with the pacifists, more extreme and alienated civil righters and miscellaneous radicals. Alongside, in a *de facto* united front, is a large proportion of the authentic—i.e., ideologized [1] rather than merely expediential [2]—Liberals, especially the Liberals of the university faculties and other verbalist occupations. What this united front is saying to the nation boils down to: Curl up and die! The nation begins to pay the price of its liaison with Liberalism. In the midst of an acute multiple crisis, Liberalism confirms its definition as the ideology of Western suicide.

Revolutionaries Are Un-American *

Scene: The American Embassy in the Republic of Cosa Nostra, a leading producer of bananas, tourist curios and revolutions. U. S. Ambassador Homer T. Pettibone looks up from his desk as a fiery-eyed young man, Simon Bolivar Juarez, storms in waiving a Cosa Nostran flag.

Juarez: Give me liberty or give me death!
Pettibone (nodding): Yes, yes. Do have a seat, Mr. Juarez. And what can I do for you?
Juarez: The corrupt and despotic dictatorship of our ruling military junta must be destroyed by the freedom-loving people of Cosa Nostra!
Pettibone: On, yes, of course. You wish to overthrow the Government. Now have you filled in the necessary application forms?

---

[1] concerned with ideology, or ideas
[2] opportunistic, concerned with self-interest or a particular end
* By Arthur Hoppe, "Revolutionaries Are Un-American," *San Francisco Chronicle*, May 12, 1965.

Juarez: Three weeks ago! Meanwhile, the iron fist of the despots has continued to crush the oppressed. . . .

Pettibone (annoyed):   I know you're impatient, Mr. Juarez, but these things take time. . . . We can't be too careful whom we allow to go around overthrowing governments, can we?

Juarez: I am a true friend of the United States and a believer in constitutional democracy!

Pettibone: That's fine, Mr. Juarez. But let me get your file. Ah, yes, your Form 1237-S-23, "Application to Overthrow the Government," seems complete. Hmmm, "Reasons for Overthrowing Government—This corrupt and despotic dictatorship must be destroyed by . . ." Well, I suppose the junta is a bit heavy-handed at times. But they are definitely anti-Communist, you'll have to admit.

Juarez: I am more so! Down with the Communists! Death to all Marxist-Leninists! Democracy forever!

Pettibone: Yes, yes, that's what you all say. But let's take a look at your Form 14-B-763(9), "Anticipated Social Reforms." Hmmm, "Modified Medicare, Moderate Aid to Education and a Limited War on Poverty." I must say, I see no problems there.

Juarez: I am a fanatic middle-of-the-roader!

Pettibone (approvingly):   I'm glad to hear that, Mr. Juarez. If you could see some of the applicants who want to overthrow governments these days. . . . Now, let's see, your three character references are here. And your psychological testing shows you to be dependable, industrious and not a whiner. Really, everything seems to be in order.

Juarez (elated):   Then you will send the Marines to help us overthrow that corrupt and despotic dictatorship?

Pettibone (shocked):   Good heavens, that would be intervention! No, Mr. Juarez, if your application is approved, it means we won't send the Marines to help their side. But, just a minute, what's this notation here about your second cousin wearing a beard? And sandals?

Juarez (blanching):   It is only because he has a weak chin and athlete's foot.

Pettibone: A bearded revolutionary! With sandals, yet! Can you imagine how that would look in the newsreels? Obviously, he's either a Castroite or a beatnik. (*Rising*) I'm afraid there's nothing I can do for you, Mr. Juarez, (*pushing a button*). Next!

The Peace Corps Against the War Corps *

President Johnson says that restoring peace and tranquillity in the Dominican Republic is an urgent objective of the United States. In setting

---

* Editorial, *San Francisco Chronicle*, May 4, 1965.

out to do that, in sending the Navy and Marines to rescue and evacuate civilians from 30 countries, the President has the unequivocal support of much congressional and public opinion in this country. Three thousand persons, he says, have been evacuated so far, and 5000 remain to be.

But what else, and whom else, are we restoring?

This is a question that weighs on the minds of other Latin American governments, some of them among our stauchest friends in the O.A.S., like the Venezuelans; they complain about the landing of the Marines. It is a question that always comes up when we land Marines in the Caribbean, because we inevitably are suspected of having political, and not merely humanitarian, objectives.

Are we duty bound to see, whenever a revolt breaks out, that it does not get into the hands of people we disapprove of?

The President has suddenly come out with an answer to this question. In his talk to the public Sunday evening, he spoke of the revolutionary movement in the Dominican Republic having taken "a tragic turn." And, he added, "Communist leaders, many of them trained in Cuba, seeing a chance to increase disorder, to gain a foothold, joined the revolution." The result, said the President, was the takeover of the revolution by a band of "Communist conspirators."

And so, although in general, "revolution in any country is a matter for that country to deal with," this does not go for revolutions run by Communists. In such cases, the revolution becomes a matter calling for hemispheric action, for "the American nations cannot, must not, and will not permit the establishment of another Communist government in the Western hemisphere."

Most Americans would say that keeping the Caribbean free of another Castro is a priority purpose of American diplomacy and defense forces. The trouble is that the Marines can't cure the troubled and desperate conditions which underlie the unrest and revolution in Santo Domingo. You cure those sorts of conditions with the Peace Corps—and we do not mean to exaggerate when we say that. Tad Szuc of the New York *Times* writes that a newspaperman, admiring the performance of the Peace Corps Americans under fire in Santo Domingo, remarked: "This is really the great American story—the Peace Corps against the war corps." If Mr. Johnson were getting his advice about what to do in Santo Domingo from the Peace Corps workers on the spot, instead of from adviser George Bundy and Secretary McNamara at the White House, we wonder if his view of the matter, and his response, might be different.

What Do You Think?

1.   You have read about the intervention in the Dominican Republic and President Johnson's explanation for that action.

With that information in mind, what is your reaction to Senator Fulbright's argument in the first reading?

2.   Some people have claimed that Senator Fulbright is blind to the dangers of communism. How would you react to such a statement?

3.   "If the non-Communist countries of Latin America or Asia do not move in concert with the United States to stop communism, in their area, then the United States should act alone." Would you agree? Why or why not?

4.   Do you agree or disagree with the evaluation of the United States' role in Arthur Hoppe's article? Explain.

ACTIVITIES FOR INVOLVEMENT

1.   Find out how the Security Council of the United Nations operates. Have your class role play the members of a Security Council meeting. The resolution to be debated, presented by Poland, is, "Resolved: That the United States' participation in the attempted overthrow of the Government of Cuba is a violation of the United Nations Charter." To have a lively debate, select the nonpermanent members of the Council according to which countries you think would have strong views on the topic.

2.   Stage a round table discussion on the question, "What should be the role of the United States in protecting the Western Hemisphere from communism?" Choose individuals to portray representatives from countries that you think would have conflicting viewpoints.

3.   Have one student act as a representative of a Latin American country and give a talk to the class on the role of the United States in Latin American affairs. He should explain which actions in the past he believes have been justifiable. Then have a second student explain to the class those actions which he believes unjustifiable. Hold a class discussion on how one decides if a policy or action is justifiable or not.

4.   Write a letter to a newspaper expressing your view on America's role in the attempted overthrow of the Castro government.

5.   Invite, if possible, the consul of some Latin American country, or a professor from a nearby university or college in your area, to discuss with the class Latin American viewpoints on the United States' role in the affairs of Latin America.

6.   Hold a mock "Meet The Press" interview in which one student portrays a State Department official giving his views of America's aid to Brigade 2056. The remainder of the class can then portray newspaper reporters questioning him.

7.   Draw a cartoon depicting any viewpoint you wish of this episode. Worry less about artistic quality and more about the idea you are trying to convey. Then let several class members hold a round-table discussion on when, and how, cartoons can be an effective means of communication.

5

Humanitarian Involvement

The Peace Corps was created by the Kennedy Administration, in 1961, to help underdeveloped countries "to meet their urgent needs for skilled manpower." Since then thousands of Peace Corpsman have contributed their skills in teaching, engineering, health, agriculture, and other fields. Will the Corpsmen's work be sustained after they leave?

The last reading in this chapter describes an example of *privately* initiated humanitarian involvement. What might be the political effects of such efforts?

1. JOHN F. KENNEDY SCHOOL NO. 1 *

This is a true story of a young man from New York State who went to a jungle community in Ecuador and became the guiding light for a new school. What were his motives?

The sounds that come from John F. Kennedy School No. 1 are the same as those that drift out of classrooms the world over—the high-pitched responses of children, an outburst of laughter, the "Yo, Professor!" of a pupil eager to recite, and the teacher's occasional, congratulatory "Very good."

But JFK No. 1 is different from other schools. Built on stilts, it is the largest structure in El Esfuerzo, Ecuador, a jungle community still too small to appear on any map. The classroom has a leaky straw roof

---

* Excerpted from Joseph Blank, "John F. Kennedy School No. 1," *Reader's Digest,* May 1965.

and a bouncy palm-bark floor. Outside, chickens, dogs and a pig wander aimlessly. Before the school opened some 15 months ago, most of the children were illiterate, and some had never held a pencil in their hands.

The *Profesor* is 27-year-old Peace Corps volunteer Edward Whalen, a tall, graceful man with closely cropped hair, a quick smile and an enthusiasm that obviously has been caught by his pupils. At 3:20 in the afternoon he led his pupils in the loud singing of the Ecuadorian national anthem, then rang the bell on his desk, signaling the end of school for the day. "See you tomorrow," he said, in English.

"See you tomorrow," chorused the pupils, ranging from 6 to 15 years old. They filed out the door and down a 12-inch-wide log with steps hewn into it.

"Two years ago I didn't know these people existed," Ed Whalen told me. "And I never imagined the thrill I would be getting from teaching."

*   *   *   *   *

During three months of study at the University of New Mexico he was given physical training, instruction in Spanish, in Ecuadorian history and customs, and in "community development"—one of the most difficult assignments in the Peace Corps. In these projects the volunteer moves into a community, lives on the same level as his neighbors, tries to learn the local problems. He is told to discover a "felt need"—a road to the highway, water piping, a schoolhouse, a better market for local goods— then help the people find an answer to the need by teaching them to work together. The volunteer has no tractors, trucks, money or other tangibles to give: only his energy, devotion and knowledge. There is need for all these in Ecuador.

For five years the Ecuadorian Institute of Agrarian Reform and Colonization had been encouraging drought-stricken farmers to migrate several hundred miles to the northwest. In the lush jungles between the Andes and the Pacific Ocean they could buy good land for about $10 an acre, on a 10-year mortgage. Some had migrated—and they needed help.

*   *   *   *   *

"The jungle excited me," Ed recalled. "But then I got into El Esfuerzo. It consisted of just three small huts and a larger hut that was a school, all built on stilts to avoid rats, snakes and the mud. There was no electricity, no water except from the river, no communication with the outside. I sat on the stepped log of the school hut, scratched my insect bites and thought, 'What have I got into? What kind of community development am I going to do, with three families, in a place like this?' "

. . . Ed visited the three houses, introduced himself and tried to explain his function. The villagers couldn't understand why an educated

American would want to leave his family and home to live in their village. They told him that 50 to 60 other huts were dispersed within a four-mile radius of the "village center." The other families had built huts on their farms, where they raised bananas and rice, and a little corn, yuca (a potato-like root), coffee and cocoa.

The next morning Ed met farmer Carlos Jirón, vice president of the village *junta.* "We built the school hut even before we began clearing the land for our farms," Jirón told Ed. "A school is the first thing. Without it, our children have no future. In fact, many fathers are here alone because they don't want to bring their families until we have a teacher for the children. We petitioned the government for one in 1961, as is the regular procedure. But there is a shortage of teachers and nothing has happened."

Ed looked around the empty, 30-by-30-foot room that was the school. It consisted of floor, roof, and palmbark walls that went halfway up the sides to let in air and light. "We'll open school," he told Jirón. . . .

Ed walked the 3½ miles back to the paved road and caught a bus. In Quito, CARE agreed to furnish him with paper and other supplies. He scrounged a few elementary-school books from the Ministry of Education. With the little money he could afford from his $100-a-month Peace Corps living allowance, he bought pencils, crayons and chalk. Then he headed back to the jungle.

On the late afternoon of November 22, 1963, a few days after Ed had opened school with a class of seven boys and girls, Maior Polanco, president of the village *junta,* walked into the school. "I have bad news," Polanco announced, serious and formal. "The radio says your President has been assassinated."

Ed was too shocked to speak.

"I bring you the condolences of your neighbors," Polanco continued. "We would like to name our school after President Kennedy because he made it possible for you to be here."

Ed nodded, still mute. The two men then composed a letter, formally registering with the Ministry of Education "The John F. Kennedy School No. 1, El Esfuerzo, Province of Pichincha."

By the end of December, Ed had 28 pupils. His Spanish had grown more fluent, and he was learning more about his youngsters. Only one had ever seen a telephone. When he asked the class to draw a picture of their homes, only four knew what to do with the crayons and paper. None of the boys owned a toy. One girl had a doll. Because they had never been encouraged to ask questions, few of the children had developed any curiosity, or understood that learning required effort on their part. But when they *did* learn something—how to write their names, or put down numbers—they became enthusiastic and were ready to learn more.

To Ed, El Esfuerzo soon became home. He slept at the schoolhouse, wrote letters and prepared his lessons at night by the light of a kerosene lamp. After checking his sleeping bag for tarantulas and beetle-size ants, he was usually in bed at nine o'clock—by which time the village was asleep, and the only sounds were unidentifiable noises from the jungle, a dog yelping, a small rat scurrying across his mosquito netting.

*   *   *   *   *

By the end of Ed's first year in El Esfuerzo, JFK No. 1 had some 70 pupils in two classes, and Ed was joined by another volunteer, Charles Vejar, who was assigned to the school until the arrival of a permanent Ecuadorian teacher. In that one year, 40 boys and girls had learned to read and write.

The community had grown from 3 to 42 homes, and many villagers were making improvements, replacing palm-bark floors and walls with milled planking. The village *junta* had opened a store that sold food staples. Three technically trained Peace Corps men, working with local volunteers, were building a bridge across the Baba River. The Ecuadorian government was breaking a gravel road through the jungle, which will enable El Esfuerzo farmers to move produce by truck to the Santo Domingo markets.

After school one day a bright-eyed nine-year-old boy remained behind and walked up to Ed's desk.

"What is it, Carlin?" Ed asked, as he shoved crayons into their cardboard containers.

The boy hesitated. Then, his eager face serious, he blurted, "Nothing, *Profesor*. I just want to say, thank you."

Ed smiled at him and said, "Thank *you*, Carlin."

"I couldn't explain it to him, but Carlin and his friends have given me more than I have given them. They have given me faith in myself. They have given me a career that I intend to follow after I leave the Peace Corps. They have given me the greatest experience of my life."

What Do You Think?

1.   Who would you say benefitted more from developing the school, Ed or the people of El Esfuerzo? Explain.

2.   Judging from this story, why do you think the United States set up the Peace Corps?

3.   If the United States wanted to help El Esfuerzo build a school, would it not have been better to have sent skilled construction workers, materials and tools so a finer building than JFK No. 1 could have been built? Why or why not?

2. SHOULD THE U. S. HAVE BECOME INVOLVED? YES!

Former Senator Kenneth Keating of New York, in eulogizing President Kennedy, cited the Peace Corps as a high point of the late President's Administration. Keating stated: " 'Youth' and 'Peace'— those two magnificent words were stamped indelibly on his Administration. In the Peace Corps, which time may show to be his finest inspiration, he joined them hand in hand. He sent them out into the world together. Was there ever before such a crusade—young America working peacefully for peace?" Is the Peace Corps a new kind of intervention?

Youth for a Better World: The Peace Corps *

Throughout the world the people of the newly developing nations are struggling for economic and social progress which reflects their deepest desires. Our own freedom, and the future of freedom around the world, depend, in a very real sense, on their ability to build growing and independent nations where men can live in dignity, liberated from the bonds of hunger, ignorance and poverty.

One of the greatest obstacles to the achievement of this goal is the lack of trained men and women with the skill to teach the young and assist in the operation of development projects, men and women with the capacity to cope with the demands of swiftly evolving economies, and with the dedication to put that capacity to work in the villages, the mountains, the towns and the factories of dozens of struggling nations.

The vast task of economic development urgently requires skilled people to do the work of the society, to help teach in the schools, construct development projects, demonstrate modern methods of sanitation in the villages, and perform a hundred other tasks calling for training and advanced knowledge.

To meet this urgent need for skilled manpower we are proposing the establishment of a Peace Corps, an organization which will recruit and train American volunteers, sending them abroad to work with the people of other nations.

This organization . . . will supplement technical advisers by offering the specific skills needed by developing nations if they are to put technical advice to work. They will help provide the skilled manpower necessary to carry out the development projects planned by the host governments, acting at a working level and serving at great personal

---

* From John F. Kennedy, *Vital Speeches*, XXVII, March 15, 1961.

sacrifice. There is little doubt that the number of those who wish to serve will be far greater than our capacity to absorb them.

*   *   *   *   *

Among the specific programs to which Peace Corps members can contribute are: teaching in primary and secondary schools, especially as part of national English-language teaching programs: participation in the worldwide program of malaria eradication; instruction and operation of public health and sanitation projects; aiding in village development through school construction and other programs; increasing rural agricultural productivity by assisting local farmers to use modern implements and techniques. The initial emphasis of these programs will be on teaching. . . .

The Peace Corps will not be limited to the young, or to college graduates. All Americans who are qualified will be welcome to join this effort. But undoubtedly the Corps will be made up primarily of young people as they complete their formal education. . . .

[T]he men and women of the Peace Corps will go only to those countries where their services and skills are genuinely needed and desired. . . .

It is essential that Peace Corpsmen and women live simply and unostentatiously among the people they have come to assist. . . .

[T]he problem of world development is not just an American problem. Let us hope that other nations will mobilize the spirit and energies and skill of their own people in some form of Peace Corps—making our effort only one step in a major international effort to increase the welfare of all men and improve understanding among nations.

What Do You Think?

1. Would you classify the Peace Corps as an example of involvement? Of intervention? Why or why not?

2. There is a domestice peace corps within the United States, known as the Volunteers in Service to America—VISTA. These volunteers help some of the thirty million poor people living in America. Should the United States send Peace Corps workers to other countries when there is so much work they could do within their own country?

The Peace Corpsman—Favorable Images *

In scores of small waves through their own zeal and ingenuity the Peace

---

* Excerpted from "The Peace Corps," *Time*, July 5, 1963. © 1963 Time, Inc. Reprinted by permission from *Time*, The Weekly News magazine.

Corpsmen have made a disproportionate number of friends for the U. S. Items:

In Ethiopia, two California school teachers—Beulah Bartlett, 65, and Blythe Monroe, 66,—moved in on an abandoned schoolhouse, white-washed it themselves, turned it into an excellent training school for native teachers. The spinster pair earned a special audience from His Imperial Majesty Haile Selassie I, and Beulah said after the meeting, "Oh, we think he's just the sweetest little man in the world." Beyond Beulah and Blythe, the Peace Corps' 200 teachers constitute half the faculty at every high school outside Addis Ababa. Since they bolstered Ethiopia's teaching force, in mid-1962, high school enrollment has nearly doubled—the greatest increase since the Ethiopian school system was started in 1908. "This," says Harris Wofford, corps representative for Ethiopia, "is what the Peace Corps was born for—to enable a country that really wants to move faster than it otherwise could."

In Cumana, Venezuela, Philip Lusardi, 27, of San Diego, asked fishermen how they were doing at catching squid which is profitable because Latin Americans consider it a delicacy, happily pay high prices for it whenever it is available. The fishermen replied that the squid catch was awful. Why? Well, squid were just too smart to be caught in wholesale numbers. Lusardi squatted in the sand, and the fishermen gathered round while he sketched diagrams of a net-and-jar technique that European fishermen use to outsmart squid. It worked in Venezuela—and Phil Lusardi is king of the beach.

In North Borneo, June Jensby, 19, a Webber, Kansas, 4-H girl, found that every long house in her bailiwick had a rusty Singer sewing machine, purchased years ago as a status symbol. But nobody knew how to work them. She scored a considerable local success by oiling the machines and giving sewing lessons. Since then, she has enlarged her curriculum to include lessons in playing volleyball, building latrines and making jam from bananas and brewing soup from cucumbers and eggs.

In Punjab, India, Peace Corpsmen arrived to find that the U. S. foreign aid program had purchased an electric wheat-grinding machine months ago for the natives' use. Unfortunately, it had sat idle ever since. Reason: the electric cord had a flat-pronged American-style plug instead of the round-pronged plug needed in India. The Peace Corpsman merely chopped off the American plug, grafted on an Indian plug, and put the machine to work to the great gratification of the whole community.

In Montalvania, Brazil, David Knoll, 20, of Chatham Center, N. Y., lives in a hovel about the size of a U. S. bathroom. Yet he has changed the whole economy of the village by persuading the peasants to pool their oxen in a farm cooperative. To Knoll, the experience has been inspiring. "After I leave the Corps, I want to do more with direct contact between people and the U. S. We've got to get down into the soil with these people. White shirts and cocktail parties aren't going to swerve them away from Communism."

In St. Lucia, a dreamy little Caribbean isle where only 14 volunteers are stationed, the local paper paid the Peace Corps its highest compliment. Said the Voice of St. Lucia: "When the Peace Corps first landed in St. Lucia, there was skepticism behind the welcoming speeches. 'Here they come,' said one socially prominent St. Lucian woman, 'straight from school to people who manage very nicely earning nothing—to teach them about refrigeration and The Star-Spangled Banner.' But today, America's Peace Corpsmen in St. Lucia have assimilated themselves into the St. Lucian society with an enthusiasm that would have made the first missionaries quake in horror. They are on first-name terms with thousands."

Corpsmen have piled up hundreds of these tiny triumphs—ranging from teaching the twist in Nyasaland to growing lettuce in Brazil to building badminton courts in Borneo. They have been treed by African buffaloes, serenaded by Filipino gigolos, adopted as sons by Southeast Asian aborigines, frightened by playful natives tossing pythons in their laps.

Western Man at His Best *

When the Peace Corps first was proposed it was ridiculed in such terms as "Kennedy's Kiddie Korps" and the "Second Children's Crusade." At the same time historian Arnold Toynbee predicted, "I believe that in the Peace Corps the non-western majority of mankind is going to meet a sample of Western Man at his best."

Time has eloquently substantiated Toynbee, for in its first five years the Peace Corps has made an impact beyond the expectations of many early supporters. In numbers alone its record is impressive: nearly 12,000 Volunteers now are at work in forty-six nations of Africa, Asia, and Latin America. Another 1,500 Volunteers are training for service overseas. By 1970, nearly 50,000 Americans will have served in and returned from Peace Corps assignments.

In more than 100,000,000 hours spent in the field Volunteers have had personal contact with some 1,300,000 students—many of whom otherwise would have had no teacher. In Colombia seventy Peace Corps Volunteers operate an educational TV program involving 7,000 teachers; it reaches 435,000 primary school children every day. The Peace Corps has expanded steadily: Volunteers in service exceeded 5,000 in 1963 and 10,000 in 1964. But demand always has exceeded supply, and to date requests from twenty countries remain unfilled.

Latin America has the largest representation of Volunteers—3,699.

---

* Excerpted from "Western Man at His Best," *Saturday Review,* April 23, 1966.
© 1966 Saturday Review, Inc.

Of these 655 are in Brazil. Other large Peace Corps contingents include 770 Volunteers in India and 760 in Nigeria. Nearly 300 vocational skills are represented, including architects, fishermen, dentists, city planners, bricklayers, civil engineers, medical technologists, stenographers, pharmacists, zoology teachers, and plumbers. Volunteers' average age is twenty-four years, but 100 Volunteers are more than fifty years old and another 100 are past age sixty. The oldest Volunteer, Eva Vinton, who is seventy-four, is a teacher in Ethiopia.

What have they accomplished?

Tangible results of their work are all about. In Tunisia, for instance, forty Peace Corps architects and city planners have designed new schools, youth centers, low-cost housing units, and municipal buildings. In Chile, a credit-union movement fostered by Peace Corps Volunteers is reported by one observer to be "blooming like wildflowers," making available moderate-interest loans in many areas for the first time. No country in which Volunteers have served is without such visible change.

Necessarily, however, many results are intangible. About half of all Volunteers teach—a stream whose currents never can be measured. In six nations in Africa alone more than half of all high school teachers with college degrees are Peace Corps Volunteers. One-third of Nigeria's students—50,000 a year—are taught by Volunteers, and in Malawi, secondary school enrollment has been tripled since arrival of the first Volunteers. Clearly no activity is more fundamental to nation-building.

Goodwill created by the Peace Corps in some countries is almost beyond price. . . . Noteworthy, . . . is the Corps' having inspired thirty nations in Europe, Latin America, Asia, and Africa to create their own international or voluntary service agencies modeled after the Peace Corps.

Nor do the effects end there. The Peace Corps training program, which encompasses fifty-seven languages, has resulted in compilation of heretofore unavailable teaching manuals. And among other unforgettable phenomena has been the effect of Peace Corps service on Volunteers themselves—a broadening and deepening which cannot help influencing national life for years to come. This growth is apparent in writings such as these:

From Volunteer Hayward Allen in Ethiopia—"Our original excitement and enthusiasm have been somewhat tempered by a year here. We have come to realize that change comes so slowly that progress, if it comes at all, seems imperceptible. The eagerness is replaced by colder ways of looking at the world, and the youthful vigor and idealism become hardened with a day-to-day job."

From Patricia MacDermot in the Philippines—"You cannot imagine the gulf between East and West, and it makes me laugh now to think that I expected to bridge it with a smile and a handshake."

From David Roseborough in Malaysia—"This is probably the most beautiful place on earth. . . . But after you've been here awhile you find something much more beautiful than rice paddies and groves of rubber trees . . . It is a very basic joy with life that I wish I could take back and inject into America."

What Do You Think?

1. What qualities do you think a Peace Corpsman should have?
2. Would it be consistent to maintain the Peace Corps while following an isolationist policy? Explain.

3. SHOULD THE UNITED STATES HAVE BECOME INVOLVED? NO!

Adverse opinion of the Peace Corps centers around the problems the Corps has run into and the shortcomings that became evident after the Corps went into operation. The Peace Corps has been criticized, but few have advocated its abolition. As you read the following selections, ask yourself how the problems could have been avoided. Might the Peace Corps do more harm than good?

Experiences in Somalia *

EVERYTHING WENT WRONG

It is difficult to think of a single thing that could have gone wrong with the Peace Corps program, that did not. From beginning to end, the Somalia One experience assumes the proportions of a case study in how *not* to conduct a Peace Corps operation.

INADEQUATE TRAINING

Fifty Peace Corps trainees entered the training program at New York University in the spring of 1962. All were earmarked for teaching jobs in Somalia. Unfortunately, the training program did not provide the kind of intensive background on the culture of the host country that is so vital to each individual's understanding and eventual adaptation. While the Peace Corps attempted to obtain properly qualified teachers, it nonetheless confronted the stubborn fact that experts on Somalia are scarce. As a consequence, few of those involved in the training program had had any previous experience in the country. And of those who did, most were

---

* Excerpted from Robert Textor (ed.), *Cultural Frontiers of the Peace Corps,* Cambridge, Mass.: M.I.T. Press, 1966.

familiar only with the former Italian Somaliland—despite the fact that the great majority of the PCVs were to be assigned to schools in former British Somaliland, an area that differs administratively and to some extent culturally from the former Italian area.

As a consequence, Volunteers were not informed of a number of significant factors. They were not told, for example, that under the influence of Egyptian propaganda Somalis were likely to voice anti-Semitic notions and attitudes. As a result some Volunteers were later surprised and deeply hurt. One personable Jewish couple, for instance, became very friendly with a Somali official and entertained him often at dinner. One evening after dinner the official innocently remarked that while Somalis could get along with anyone, the only people they really hated were the Jews. Although the wife later broke down in tears, the couple contained their reactions so well at the time that the incident passed unnoticed. But the spiritual wound never healed completely.

The training program also failed to inform PCVs that some Somalis tend to look down on Negroes. This also left certain Negro Volunteers unprepared to make the necessary adjustment, and led to the same kind of painful surprise. . . .

LOGISTICAL FAILURES

Housing for those few Volunteers working in the South was a problem. Although the agreement with the Somali government stated that housing was to be provided, a number of Volunteers were unable to find space. Peace Corps officials took this as a sign that the government was indifferent, and unwilling to support Peace Corps activities. What they failed to realize was that the Volunteers were not being treated differently from anyone else. In the early days of independence, expatriate and Somali civil servants were attempting to integrate the inherited British and Italian administrative systems and inefficiency was at a peak. Somalis employed by their own government often went for months, or even years, before they got on the payroll. In this situation it was unrealistic to expect the Somali government to handle Peace Corps matters with great efficiency.

JOB FRUSTRATION

In meeting their teaching responsibilities in the classroom, many Volunteers at first tried to establish rapport with their students by being "regular guys." Somali students quickly sensed the Volunteers' insecurity and lack of experience, took advantage of their good-will, and tested them to the limits. Classroom discipline soon became a major problem, in a few cases breaking down completely. Many Volunteers responded by administering corporal punishment—or calling on school officials to do so.

Volunteers were plagued by other frustrations as well. Schools lacked books and supplies. Even basic necessities, such as pencils and paper, were often completely lacking. At times the available books would be locked up in the school library by the principal, who would then disappear into the capital city hundreds of miles away, to remain for weeks or months at a time. Nor did it help matters when teaching aids, promised by Peace Corps/Washington, would sometimes fail to materialize. . . .

LONELINESS AND BOREDOM

Perhaps the most serious problem of all was simply that there was not enough adventure or diversion. To their surprise, Volunteers discovered that being a teacher was in many respects a tedious, tiring, and humdrum round of activities, almost completely devoid of romance or adventure. Life was a tread-mill existence: prepare lessons, go to school, teach classes, go home; day after day after dismal day. And in the remote outposts there was hardly a diversion to lighten the load: no bar or restaurant, no dance hall, no girls to date, not even the lowest-grade movie to help while away a dull weekend.

PSYCHOLOGICAL ISOLATION

The daily tedium, the loneliness and isolation of distant posts, might have been bearable if somebody had seemed to appreciate their efforts. But this was not the case. Their Somali teacher colleagues and other Somali officials seemed apathetic to say the least. Their own students were defiant and seemed highly unappreciative. The Volunteers felt that all was useless and pointless, that they were accomplishing litttle or nothing of any value. Their self-esteem was deeply wounded. They had started out as enthusiastic idealists, and now their morale was slipping ever lower.

They needed somebody to talk to, somebody who could give them psychological and logistic support, somebody who could help them make sense out of the local culture. But there was nobody. Clearly, their Representative was not such a person. And Washington was too far away.

"Foul-Ups" and "Dumb" Decisions *

[Peace Corpsman] have also been the victims of inexcusable administrative foul-ups. A batch of young nurses was sent to a medical aid station in Bolivia only to find that the place was to be closed down shortly after they arrived. Mrs. Frances Cunha, 74, a California walnut-farm owner, was sent to the dust bowl near the São Francisco river valley in Brazil to help nurture the cashew and Brazil-nut trees. She quickly discovered that nut trees had never been grown there. Again, a group of volunteers was posted to a scruffy village in Nepal, found that no one knew they were coming, who they were or what they were supposed to do. They spent the

---

* Excerpted from "The Peace Corps," *Time,* July 5, 1963. © 1963 Time, Inc.

night huddled grimly beneath flimsy blankets in a bare, cold house, finally broke up in laughter when a voice piped up, "Any more bright ideas, Mr. Kennedy?"

The Corps' largest program is in the Philippine Islands, where there are 600 "teachers' aides." It has also been one of the least satisfying—at least to the volunteers. Most of them are young liberal-arts college graduates without teaching experience. They were sent in to help out Filipino teachers in village classrooms, and no one knew exactly what they were supposed to do when they got there. Some took over classes almost entirely; others stood around to help out with an English translation now and then. Generally, the Philippines volunteers can see no real progress. Says one corpsman: "We read about a volunteer in South America who has made 3,000,000 bricks or built a bridge, and we feel discouraged. We ask: 'What have we done?' "

But not all of the corpsmen agree with that assessment of progress. Many of them charged into Colombia 21 months ago, full of enthusiasm, and ran full tilt into a stone wall of local government inertia. Michael Wilson, 26, of Hinsdale, Ill., says he waited two months for the Colombian Public Works Ministry to lend him a bulldozer for one day to grade a road. But the day it arrived was a national holiday, and the whole town was drunk. "It wasn't deliberate. Just dumb, man," says Wilson. And Bruce Lane, 25, of Austin, Texas, was totally soured by his experiences: "I came here two years ago with the attitude of a social worker who was going to help the country's peasants. Now I feel to hell with 'em."

What Do You Think?

1. Should Peace Corps candidates be screened? Why or why not? If yes, what criteria should be used?
2. What do you think should be included in the Peace Corps training program?
3. Should the Peace Corps have been withdrawn from Somalia? Why or why not?

Bring Home the Peace Corps

Few people speak against the Peace Corps. On the whole the Corps is looked upon as a well-intentioned humanitarian effort. To some extent it is just that. But the Peace Corps has some serious shortcomings that raise the question about continuing the program. We must not be blinded by the many favorable things we hear and read. We owe it to our own people, as well as to the people in other lands, to open our eyes to the other side of the picture.

Millions of Americans need help. Poverty, ignorance, disease, and other human sufferings still exist in the United States. Charity begins at home. Why should we spend our money and human resources in other countries when we need them here? The Peace Corps has operated long enough now to give the peoples of other lands the idea of how to carry on the program. The time has come to call the Corpsmen home and incorporate them into the VISTA program. America in the 1970's will need VISTA far more than she will need the Peace Corps.

It is unfortunate that sometimes the Peace Corps has operated against America's interests. In Africa, Asia, and Latin America the program has been carried out in countries that receive aid from the Soviet Union and Communist China, and look favorably upon them. Peace Corpsmen train local workers, who then work on projects financed by Russia. In the end the Russians have tangible products to show off and win popularity and the support of the particular government involved. In Vietnam Peace Corpsmen help set up villages, which later become bases for the Viet Cong. American soldiers have to pay the price in blood for the Peace Corps' work.

We often hear about Peace Corpsmen making friends for America. How about the enemies they make? Corpsmen ignorant of local customs and traditions often create more antagonism than friendships. Young Corpsmen, fresh out of college, high in spirit and ambition, but low in maturity and understanding, start projects in which the people they are supposed to help are not yet ready to participate. The Corpsmen become disillusioned, and the people become disenchanted with these Americans. Administrative mistakes and bureaucratic red tape have fouled up the program in too many cases. On many occasions the wrong people and the wrong supplies have been sent to the wrong places. One may wonder what image of Americans result from the many unfortunate episodes that have occurred—is the "Ugly American" being perpetuated?

The idea behind the Peace Corps was good. But experience now seems to tell us that the Corps has done some harm abroad. Many of the Corpsmen could be useful here at home, and their mistakes would not harm the nation's image abroad. The Peace Corps should be brought home.

What Do You Think?

1. Do you agree that in the 1970's VISTA will be more important than the Peace Corps? Why or why not?
2. Should Peace Corpsman be sent to countries that accept aid from Russia and Communist China? Why or why not?

4. A MEDICAL MISSIONARY IN LAOS *

Thomas Dooley was a young United States Navy doctor who had been sent ashore in Vietnam at the conclusion of the French Indo-China War in 1954 to help Vietnamese people who needed medical care. This experience in Vietnam changed Tom Dooley's life. He resigned from the Navy, gave up the promise of a prosperous practice in the United States, and determined to bring person-to-person medical assistance to sick and needy people in Vietnam and Laos. With a team of volunteers, he set up a hospital in Laos in 1956.

Tom Dooley died of cancer in 1961. His co-workers continued the program he had started, which eventually led to the establishment of several medical centers in Laos. As you read the excerpt below, consider the possible implications of such humanitarian service for foreign policy.

. . . On a sweltering day in August [1956] I stood in the Manila airport watching a plane glide down through the heat haze rising from the runway. It taxied around, and the door swung open, out stepped Pete Kessey, a lean and hungry-looking Texan, followed by 200-pound, barrel-chested Baker—flexing his muscles, as always—and then quiet, serious Denny Shepard. Pete and Denny were 25. Baker was still only 21. Yet they were more mature and dependable than most men twice their age.

We had about an hour's wait before leaving for Saigon, which was to be our "staging area." The boys plied me with questions. What kind of gear did you have? How had I ever high-pressured the Navy into hauling the four tons of stuff to Saigon? Where did we go from there? What kind of place was Laos? ("Yeah, man," groaned Baker. "I can see now that this means living on C-rations and holding 24-hour sick call!")

When we were back aboard the plane, the talk turned serious. I got out my map and explained that, if my plans went through, we would operate up north in the town of Nam Tha. Denny gave a long, low whistle of surprise. He had a bundle of notes and clippings, and knew as much about Laos as I did.

I told them about the flying trip I had made to Hong Kong to meet Oden Meeker, a dynamic young American who had served in Laos with CARE during the famine of 1954. Oden strongly favored the plan to operate in Nam Tha. It was a critical area, he said, the most isolated part of Laos, and politically the most vulnerable. "Those mountain people

---

* Excerpted from Tom Dooley, *The Edge of Tomorrow.* New York, N. Y.: Farrar, Straus and Giroux, 1958. Reprinted by permission Farrar, Straus and Giroux.

have rarely seen a white man," said Oden. "They have no allegiance to the central government . . ."

The boys listened solemnly. Then Baker said: "Look, Doc, you've got to level with us. What are the odds on this set-up? I'm a married man now. So is Denny . . . Besides, I never did like the sound of those Chinese prison camps."

Well, I said, the odds were about standard for that part of the world. No better, no worse. We'd been in tough spots before, but we had done our jobs, and come through with our hides intact. Baker hooted.

"Oh, we sure did—only you forget that we had the U. S. Navy back of us last time!"

I let that pass, and switched to the kind of job we had to do. We wouldn't be "showing the flag" so much this time. . . . We'd be showing American face to a lot of Asians who had been told that American white men didn't give a damn. I . . . invited them to think of what we could accomplish by working among people on the village level in Laos.

Pete Kessey spoke up. "Doc, it looks to me like you expect to accomplish an awful lot in a short time. You know we only signed on for six months. You think we can do a job by then? And what happens to you when we pull out?"

That was the one part of the plan that had me worried, but I couldn't admit it. After six months, I said, I'd be able to play it by ear. . . . Maybe I could train a few young Lao to serve as assistants. And I also had a scheme in mind for getting a few replacements from the States.

They sensed that I was whistling in the dark. Baker declared that this was the screwiest part of the whole set-up. Pete shook his head. I was glad when Denny broke it up.

"This is one devil of a time to be talking about going home," he said. "We're not even there yet!"

United States Ambassador Parsons was emphatic in opposing my plan to go to Nam Tha. Indeed, he wanted my team to stay as far away from the China border as possible. The political situation in Laos was touchy; conditions in the north might even become explosive. No matter what I did or said or even could prove, it was inevitable that people would suspect me of being an American espionage agent. . . . In the north the Communists would do everything possible to spread the word that I was a spy. . . . If I or any of my men became involved in an "incident," the entire American position in Laos would be jeopardized.

. . . I asked him where he thought my team might operate. We went over to the map, and he indicated the area around Vang Vieng, about 120 miles north of the capital but still far south of the China border. During the Indo-China war, he said, Vang Vieng had been captured by the Communists; conditions there were still pretty bad. . . . So Vang Vieng it was.

. . . About half the people of Vang Vieng were out to meet us when the trucks and jeeps of Operation Laos arrived in town. Ojisan [an old villager] had spread the word that we were white medicine-men bringing powerful remedies to the people. Hence many of the women and children came with gifts of flowers, cucumbers and oranges.

We found the Lao dispensary at one end of the square. . . . It was a low, whitewashed building of three rooms. . . .

Norman Baker was our chief construction man, . . . and under his direction the boys went to work converting the dispensary into a small hospital. They swept, swabbed, disinfected, and then whitewashed. With the aid of a half-dozen coolies, we cleared the surrounding yard . . . of debris, cow dung, and heaps of foul bandages and dressings. Then we built a fence to keep out the wandering water buffalo.

The medical supplies were uncrated, and Baker did an ingenious job of converting the empty boxes into tables and benches, and cabinets in which to store our pharmaceuticals. Then we borrowed some cots from the local detachment of the Royal Lao army. When these had been de-loused and repaired, we set them up in the room which was to serve as the ward.

We never announced sick-call, and we needed no publicity. Only a few days after our arrival we were awakened one morning by sounds that were to become a familiar part of every dawn—the howls of sickly babies, the hacking coughs of tubercular mothers. Why wait on line at the hospital, when you can camp on the doctor's front porch!

Frankly, I was overwhelmed by the horrible health conditions we found. There were yaws, tuberculosis, pneumonia, malaria and diseases far more heartrending. I was appalled by the sight of so many women mutilated and crippled in childbirth, and by the many traumatic injuries long neglected and horribly infected.

The hideous yaws we could cure with the "1-2-3 treatment": one shot of penicillin, two bars of soap and three days! There was little we could do about the tuberculosis, except to control the paroxysms of cough-ing with cough syrup; for it is the racking cough that frequently causes pneumonia and hastens the tubercular's death.

. . . More than 50 per cent of the patients we saw had malaria. Usually these people had survived many attacks of the disease, and achieved a certain immunity; but they were left with greatly enlarged spleens. When the spleen is diseased, the blood loses some of its ability to coagulate, and the slightest cut or bruise can cause a serious hemorrhage. So we pumped vitamins into almost every patient we saw.

One morning at sick call a poor woman pushed a huge, smelly bundle of rags into my arms. I peeled away the layers of clothing and uncovered a baby about a year old. He was a hideous sight. His abdomen looked like an overblown balloon that was about to burst, the chest looked like a miniature birdcage. There was a tiny monkey face with wild, unseeing eyes. Kwashiorkor's disease! And this was only the first of countless cases we were to encounter in Laos.

Kwashiorkor's disease, fairly common in the tropics, is not caused by infection but by ignorance. It is the grotesque result of malnutrition. Metabolism fails, muscles waste away, liver and spleen are enlarged, the abdomen swells, and the heart and circulation are damaged. The end result is death.

But this horrible process is reversible if caught in time. This was an extreme case. The mother had fallen ill and was unable to nurse her baby; so, from the age of about six months, the child was fed only rice and water.

Successful treatment of Kwashiorkor depends upon extremely cautious feeding so as not to overtax the weakened system. We injected vitamins, then used the wonderful protein powder called MPF (Multi-Purpose Food) . . . MPF can be used in many ways. Two ounces of the powder made into a broth, for example, provide protein equivalent to a steak dinner. We put the baby on a diet of MPF solution and fruit juices and got remarkable results. The damage to the heart and eyes, unfortunately, was irreversible. But the child lived.

That night I told the boys that we were adding another project to our schedule. We were starting regular classes, open to all, in nutrition, hygiene and similar matters.

What Do You Think?

1. Was Tom Dooley's work of value to the United States? If so, how?

2. There is a shortage of doctors in many parts of the United States. Suppose you were a member of a small community that needed a physician. What arguments would you use to try and persuade Dooley to remain in the United States?

ACTIVITIES FOR INVOLVEMENT

1. Invite a Peace Corps worker to class to tell about his experiences. Present him with a number of the incidents, both pro and con, that you have read about in this chapter. How does he react? How would you explain his reactions? What future does he foresee for the Peace Corps?

2. The American Friends Service Committee is a nongovernmental organization that does Peace Corps-type work overseas. Contact them for a speaker to discuss their overseas and Indian reservation projects. What are the Committee's major concerns? Would you consider this group interventionist?

3.   Have you ever thought about being a foster parent? For less than $200 a year it is possible to help a child in Latin America, Africa, or Asia to get the food, clothing, and education he needs to grow up to live a normal life. You can do this through the Foster Parent's Plan, Inc., 352 Park Avenue South, New York 10010, or through the Save the Children Federation, Post Road, Norwalk, Connecticut, 06852. You can make it a class or a school project to earn the money.

4.   If possible, invite a member of the consular corps from a country that has received Peace Corps workers (or perhaps someone who has visited the country), to speak to the class on what the Peace Corps has done in his country, his impressions of the volunteers, and how his people feel about them.

5.   Hold a mock "Meet the Press" interview in which one student portrays the Director of the Peace Corps and the remainder of the class portrays the inquiring reporters.

6.   Either debate or write a brief essay on one of the following topics:

a. Resolved: That a young man should be allowed to serve in the Peace Corps in lieu of military service.
b. Resolved: That only college-trained people should be accepted by the Peace Corps.
c. Resolved: That there should be compulsory national service for all youth between 18 and 25. (National service means working in the military, the Peace Corps, or VISTA.)

7.   Listed below are a number of characteristics that have been suggested as desirable for Peace Corps trainees to possess:

kind	low anxiety level
tolerant	intelligent
brave	deep interest in other cultures
fluent in language of country to which being sent	humanistic
ascetic	self-sacrificing
stoic	non-materialistic
patient	open-minded
adventurous	flexible
	good sense of humor

Which do you think are the five *most* important? *Least* important? Defend your choice.

8.   Invite a speaker from the local chapter of the American Medical Association in your community to inform the class on what American physicians are doing to promote better health programs around the world.

6

Economic Involvement

American companies are branching out. They are expanding not only throughout the United States but also into other countries. Billions of dollars have been flowing to Europe and Latin America to open new companies or buy out established ones. Why? What is attracting American money to foreign lands? What effect does large American investment have on these countries?

1. THE GREAT AMERICAN PURCHASE *

The following Newsweek *article describes the expansion of American companies into Europe. Is this a new form of economic colonialism?*

The gentleman's suit is immaculately European and his French is faultlessly French. His calling card reveals him to be *Directeur Général, Banque de Commerce, Bruxelles.* But, appearances to the contrary, Francis L. Mason is an American and a vice president of New York's Chase Manhattan Bank, which just happens to own a 50 per cent interest in the Banque de Commerce. There are hundreds like him, field commanders in the newest theater of American business operations: The economic invasion of Western Europe.

The number of financial beachheads opened up and the amount of industrial high ground already captured in this invasion is staggering to behold. Chicago's First National Bank has bought a stake in Holland's big (50 branches) N. V. Slavenburg Bank. Late last year, Paris's Banque Mobiliere et Industreille changed hands; it now belongs to New York's Blyth & Co. And Chase Manhattan, thanks to a steady diet of take-overs, has become the second-largest commercial bank in all of France.

---

* Excerpted from "Great American Purchase," *Newsweek,* February 27, 1967.

Europe's bustling assembly lines, too, are increasingly apt to be owned by Americans. Companies controlled by Detroit now build more than half the automobiles manufactured in Britain and 30 per cent of all Western European models. More than half the drugs supplied to Britain's National Health Service come either from American subsidiaries or directly from the U. S. ITT, the largest (100,000 employees) U. S. firm in Europe, has cornered 30 per cent of Europe's telephone market; IBM makes well over half the Continent's computers, and General Electric and Honeywell account for most of the rest.

Even the proud towers of the French perfume industry are beginning to topple before the American siege. Revlon has absorbed both Balmain and Raphael; Pfizer owns Coty; Max Factor owns Corday; and this week the famous Parfums Carons is likely to sell a controlling interest to A. H. Tobins Co., a pharmaceutical firm in Richmond, Va. . . .

[T]he surge of American ownership in Europe is growing at the astounding pace of $11 million a day—or $4 billion a year. In 1964, when the American business stake in Europe passed the $12 billion mark, most experts predicted it would soon level off. Today, it is about to top $20 billion—and is still climbing.

To a considerable extent, the success of America's invasion is due simply to the U. S. firms' advantage in size and money. Everything European is dwarfed by the mastodons of American manufacturing, backed by the resources of the most opulent money market in the world. In a number of cases, European companies have opened their doors to American ownership only because there seemed no way to raise the funds they needed within Europe. And wealth also means flexibility. "Americans can afford to run at a loss much longer than we can," says a prominent French businessman. They are also far more capable of risking enormous sums to launch a new product in the increasingly affluent European market.

But America's size and riches have combined to create an even more potent weapon in her favor—the so-called "technology gap." . . .

Technological research and development has undoubtedly given the U.S. a tremendous advantage. Since 1955, American business and the Federal government between them have been boosting R & D outlays by about 16 per cent annually, so that they are now heading rapidly toward the $30 billion-a-year mark. All of Western Europe, by contrast, is spending less than a third of that amount, and with a minimum of coordination of effort between countries.

What Do You Think?

1. There are about four million unemployed people in the United States. Should American companies be concerned about this? What might they do?

   2.   Should the American government regulate overseas investments by American companies? Why or why not?

   3.   How should foreign countries react to American investments?
Why?

2. SHOULD THE UNITED STATES HAVE BECOME INVOLVED? YES!

*The following readings indicate that the expansion of United States
business enterprises into less-developed foreign lands provides a great
opportunity for these areas. What advantages and disadvantages can
you forsee for the countries involved?*

Planting Profits in Economic Deserts *

*This example concerns an American paper company that develops
factories in foreign lands—and then pulls out.*

Some 1000 Tunisians, including President Habib Bourguiba and other
dignitaries, gathered in the town of Kasserine at the edge of the Sahara
Desert for the ceremonial occasion. Amid speeches and flapping flags, they
were launching Tunisia's first pulp mill: the $13-million plant of the Societe
Nationale Tunisienne de Cellulose. As everyone watched, bales of esparto
grass, a tough, fibrous plant which has long been used in the manufacture
of rope, baskets and paper, were fed into the mill's gleaming new machinery. The esparto emerged two hours later as high-grade pulp for writing
paper—the first of 80 tons now produced daily at the mill.

Up to a few months before that November day in 1963, the area
around Kasserine Pass, . . . had been close to desert, economically and
physically. The esparto was harvested by Bedouins for export only, and
the importing of paper drained precious foreign currency from the treasury. Now the paper mill's technicians, graduates of the local high school
who formerly had bleak prospects as agricultural workers and share-
croppers, operate the intricate U. S.-built machines with all the skill of
Detroit assembly-line veterans. Their chief, a native engineer, today heads
420 employees and bears full responsibility for the mill's production.

All these changes were effected by an enterprising American firm
named Parsons & Whittemore, which has been in the pulp and paper
business for more than 110 years. One of the largest privately owned
companies headquartered in the United States—it and its affiliates have

---

* Excerpted from Paul Deutschman. "They Plant Profits in Economic Deserts."
Reader's Digest, January, 1967.

11,000 employees, and branches in 22 countries—P. & W. has developed an unusual way of setting up profitable businesses abroad. Starting from scratch, the company builds pulp and paper plants, trains workers and managers and, at a designated date, "turns over the keys" to the new owners. And the factories are *guaranteed* to be put into profit-making operation.

P. & W. started creating these "packaged plants" in 1958 in pre-Castro Cuba. It has now developed 26 profitable projects in countries as far apart as Argentina and Egypt, Ethiopia and South Vietnam, Mexico and India. These represent a total capital investment of $432 million. In addition, 15 turn-key projects are presently under way, and at least 25 others are planned.

Several U. S. companies have been successful with such plants in under-developed nations—with fertilizer factories, textile mills and cement plants. None, however, proceeds in quite the same way as Parsons & Whittemore. It handles every step of setting up a plant—from financing to guaranteed production. And in places where ordinary timber is not available for pulp, it supplies speedy modern machines that can be used on other materials such as esparto, straw or bagasse (the fibrous waste product of sugar cane).

Why does Parsons & Whittemore do all this? "To make a profit," Karl Landegger, its owner, told me. . . .

During the early 1950's, Landegger received many inquiries about Black-Clawson machines from newly industrializing nations—but few sales resulted. "We soon realized," Landegger told me, "that we could sell a mill only as a 'package.' It's difficult to sell pieces of equipment to someone who doesn't know what to do with them. Who would run the machines? What about the mill's financing? Ten million dollars is a sizable outlay for some less-developed countries. And many countries that needed paper mills had no timber. That was how we became involved with other materials." . . .

A project usually starts when P. & W. is approached by local businessmen and asked to make a feasibility study—a systematic assessment of all the pros and cons involved in operating a paper mill in a particular country. Such a study may last from two weeks to two years and cost up to $250,000. Then, if the project is approved, the two parties work out a "collaboration agreement." This may mean a simple fee for P. & W., a partnership arrangement, a stock participation in the future mill, or even an obligation to manage the mill for a specified time.

Then P. & W. tackles the financing. Besides the company and its client, other participants may include the local government and any number of private investors, ranging from a king, as in Thailand, to prosperous farmers and small businessmen, as in India. Usually there is some U. S.

government backing, typically via Export-Import Bank or Agency for International Development loans, which require that the newly ordained mill purchase all possible imports of machinery and services in the United States. Investors could hardly undertake such costly projects without these loans. . . .

[T]he most important aspects of a turn-key project are its unwritten clauses, which depend basically on people—working, learning and aspiring together. At least 11,000 locals have had to be trained as technicians, some on the spot, some in the United States or other paper-manufacturing countries. "The biggest difficulty in developing a new industry," Landegger told me, "is the development of people. It takes two years to build a paper mill, but much longer to train an industrial worker. In most of the areas where we've built, the only industrial equipment a worker has seen previously is a light bulb—and he's in awe of that."

There is also the problem of reaching a meeting of minds with local government. "Any enterprise," Landegger said, "has to create capital for its own expansion. But sometimes a government of one of the less-developed countries will see a factory creating capital—that is, making a profit—and immediately there will be a new tax law designed to keep the factory from holding onto its profit. What this can do is prolong the country's dependence on foreign aid." . . .

The turn-keys also help move many less-developed countries toward economic independence. By contributing to the growth of a local paper industry, a P. & W. mill makes it less necessary for that country to import paper and pulp. This releases foreign exchange—U. S. dollars and other hard currencies—for imports like machine tools and crucial raw materials. . . .

All this means a continuously increasing number of new jobs, new skills, new opportunities. And in the process it creates the most important spin-off of all—the spin-off of man's ever-soaring hopes for the future.

What Do You Think?

1. Is P. & W. exploiting the countries where it sets up its mills? Explain.

2. How do you *feel* about P. & W.'s activities in Tunisia? Explain.

3. Would you call P. & W.'s activities economic intervention? Explain.

"U. S. Businessmen on the Move" *

*A new brand of capitalism is replacing the 19th Century concept of
"exploitive capitalism." What is this new brand? How does it differ
from exploitation? To whom is it beneficial? Harmful?*

To American eyes, it was a strange sight indeed. Down in a deep pit
a Moslem *mullah* priest was sacrificing a ram to—of all things—the future
success of the Chrysler Corporation.

It had all begun when Chrysler scheduled a cornerstone-laying for its
new assembly plant in Istanbul, Turkey. After a few speeches in the tradi-
tional American manner, the Moslem priest took over. He descended into
the pit with a large white ram, its horns and hoofs painted gold. Just as
the ram was sacrified, the sun broke through the clouds. The Moslems
were delighted at this good omen for the future of the plant. There had
been no sunshine for two weeks before.

With this strange mixing of American and Turkish customs, a new
U. S. business venture abroad was launched. Not all are begun quite as
exotically. Yet they occur with such frequency and in so many countries
that they make up a large—and ever-growing—portion of the world's
economic scene. According to an estimate by the *Wall Street Journal,*
U. S. businessmen have invested about $100,000,000,000 in foreign coun-
tries. (That's roughly twice the total the rest of the world has invested in
the U. S.)

Caring for these investments and searching for new possibilities are
approximately 25,000 enterprising American businessmen. They can be
found almost everywhere on the globe—even behind the Iron Curtain.
Nearly half of them are connected in some way with the oil industry. Next
in size are those dealing more generally with manufacturing and sales of
various products, closely followed by engineers.

The companies they represent range in size from the giant Creole
Petroleum Company, which is developing the oil resources of Venezuela,
to a one-man trader exporting handicrafts from a small African country.

"American businessmen abroad," . . . "are selling insurance and
bulldozers, mining quicksilver and cutting timber, building dams and laying
pipe. They are found in the capital cities of the world, or 'out on the boon-
docks.' They go abroad to live, and set up business operations, and to manage those operations in a manner designed to fulfill the basic requirement
of any commercial enterprise: to earn a profit."

Most countries welcome them. The investment capital they bring is

---

* Excerpted from "U. S. Businessmen on the Move." *Senior Scholastic,* March
11, 1965. By permission *Senior Scholastic.* © 1965 Scholastic Magazines, Inc.

often not available on the domestic market of these countries. The Americans also usually possess technical skills which the local businessman does not have. And, once in operation, the successful American-owned enterprise pays local taxes—which often provide the money for a local government to pursue its own development plans. Then, too, the American-owned enterprises often pay their workers wages higher than the going rate in local industry.

It sounds like a mutually profitable arrangement—and in most cases it is. Yet U. S. businessmen are not always welcomed with open arms. Here's why:

Many people, especially in the less-developed countries, view the U. S. businessman as a modern-day version of a 19th-century colonialist. Propaganda from some sources, mostly leftist, goes this way: "North American capitalists want to keep the people here in poverty so they can take over the country's minerals and metals; they care *only* for their profits." This theory bears little relation to the facts. Yet U. S. businessmen overseas sometimes find themselves the object of local hostility built upon it.

Pressure on local governments to "do something about U. S. 'economic imperialism' " has sometimes led to restrictions on U. S. businessmen, higher taxes, or—in extreme cases—expropriation (government takeover of the business). In Cuba, for example, Castro's government expropriated more than $1.5 billion worth of U. S. property in two years.

Many leading U. S. businessmen today urge a more positive approach to combat these myths. A leading exponent is David Rockefeller, president of the Chase Manhattan Bank of New York. Among his other activities, Rockefeller has helped organize the International Executive Service Corps, a kind of "businessmen's peace corps." The purpose of the corps is to provide developing countries with experienced executives who can get new enterprises started and then train local businessmen to manage them.

Writes Rockefeller: "Through our actions we must demonstrate that 'exploitive capitalism' is a thing of the past. We must demonstrate that there has evolved a new brand of capitalism based on the concept of a fair profit for free enterprise."

Many U. S. companies have already learned this lesson well: Kaiser Industries, for example, has built automobile companies in Brazil and Argentina and sold most of the stock in these companies to Latin Americans. And, instead of importing parts from the U. S., Kaiser sought out local industries. The company also established educational programs to train skilled technicians for its industries. Men who showed promise were sent abroad for further training. Today all but a handful of Kaiser's employees in these two countries are Brazilians or Argentinians.

Kaiser is not the only U. S. firm to employ such progressive techniques abroad. The list of other companies involved in social projects in host countries is long and includes Sears, Roebuck and Co., in Mexico; Creole Petroleum in Venezuela; and Arabian-American Oil in Saudi Arabia.

What Do You Think?

1. Do American companies have obligations to the countries wherein they make investments? Explain.
2. American companies usually pay their workers overseas less than they pay an American worker for doing comparable work. How might this practice be defended? Argued against?
3. It has been argued that expropriation of foreign-owned property is the same as stealing. Would you agree or disagree? Explain.

3. SHOULD THE UNITED STATES HAVE BECOME INVOLVED? NO!

Investing in foreign countries involves more than just making profits; there is the problem of adjusting to the local political and economic systems. Under the American political-economic system, business enterprises have more freedom than they do under many semi-socialist systems abroad, where the governments exercise greater regulation of prices, wages, and production. What sort of conflicts might develop?

Political and Social Impact *

The following article indicates how individualistic American business practices may sometimes lead to difficulties when applied abroad. How can these problems be avoided?

American business is investing billions of dollars in industries abroad and moving its plants to foreign lands. . . .

During the years 1957 to 1960, production volume of American firms manufacturing overseas increased from $18.3 billion to $24 billion. General Motors and Ford now control 40 per cent of the British automobile industry and 30 per cent of West Germany. Chrysler has recently gained control of 63 per cent of Simca, a major French automobile manufacturer.

---

* Excerpted from Frank Kowalski, "American Plants Abroad," *The Nation,* October 5, 1963.

In 1951, General Motors manufactured 200,000 GM cars and trucks in its overseas plants. In 1960, this production went up to 800,000 vehicles. American manufacturers now control the major output in Europe of tractors, telephone and telegraph equipment, farm machinery, ball bearings, sewing machines, electronics and photographic materials and equipment. It is reported that in five years, 3,500 American industries have moved abroad; more than 50 per cent have chosen Western Europe. . . .

While the economics of the huge transfer of dollars and plants has received considerable attention, we are just beginning to see the political and social impact of these massive movements. Along with the blessings of rapid business expansions, new jobs and more money have come social dislocations and political grumblings. For the laissez-faire American business operations do not always mesh comfortably into the semi-socialistic economies of Latin America or Europe.

When General Motors (France) a year ago suddenly laid off 685 workmen at its Frigidaire plant in a suburb of Paris, it brought an avalanche of criticism upon itself and American operations in general. The French have a comprehensive national economic plan which enjoys general support from the people, the unions and the business community. Right or wrong, the French have credited their economic plan for their prosperity.

The layoff of 685 workers obviously did not affect the French economy, but French industry operates closely with the authorities. A French company would have consulted and negotiated with the officials concerned before closing its doors to its workers. General Motors, according to reports, executed the lay-off in a matter of hours and with no outside consultations. The French newspapers were incensed at the "irresponsible" action of this American company, and the Minister of Industries lodged an angry protest with General Motors. The grumblings went on for many days throughout France and tempers were further agitated when Remington Rand laid off 1,200 workers at its plant near Lyons.

In a different way, the Libby canning project has collided with important socio-political forces in France. In this case the French Government, after repeated efforts to get French interests to organize a modern canning industry, finally gave up and invited Libby to take over. The reaction from French farm organizations, Socialists, Communists and left-wing Gaullists was violent. The government had spent more than $160 million in developing the Bas-Rhone-Languedoc area and these French groups saw the Libby company reaping a harvest sown with French francs. As viewed by these French groups, the American company was not only an economic competitor, but was undermining fundamental French aspirations to establish a nationalized canning enterprise or a state-supported cooperative.

Absentee Landlords *

Another complaint frequently heard is that the "parent company" makes the decisions and conducts all research in the United States, thus depriving the branches of scientific stimulation and administrative control.

. . .an increasing number of responsible Europeans, peering into the future, feel ominously threatened with the fate that has already befallen Canada, where 60 per cent of all productive capacity is now U. S.-controlled. "First Louisiana, then Alaska, now Canada—and, next, Europe," ruminated a Belgian chemical executive recently, only half in jest. What bothers Europeans most is their belief that business decisions crucial to their economic welfare are being made by parent companies in Phoenix, Detroit and Los Angeles, where U. S. domestic factors are still the main consideration, rather than in Brussels, Paris or Frankfurt, where European interests might prevail. And sometimes—though by no means always—this belief is justified. Many of the U. S. giants, for example, carry out all their basic research at home, thus depriving their European subsidiaries of the prestige and stimulus of work on the technological frontiers. . . .

Today, American investments in France may be only an irritant to its economic planners, but tomorrow if a Labour government were installed in England, a socialistic British economy might have to come to serious grips with laissez-faire American operations in that country.. . .

What Do You Think?

1. Should American companies have to submit to foreign controls? Explain your reasoning.
2. "American manufacturers now control the major output in Europe of tractors, telephone and telegraph equipment, farm machinery, ball bearings, sewing machines, electronics, and photographic materials and equipment." How might this affect the European economy?

A European Is Alarmed *

The large American penetration into Europe's economy has alarmed some Europeans. They fear that Europe's economic position will not keep pace with the growing economies of the United States and the

---

* Excerpted from "Great American Purchase," *Newsweek,* February 27, 1967. Copyright Newsweek, Inc., 1967.
* "The American Challenge," *Time,* November 24, 1967. © Time, Inc.

Soviet Union. Jean-Jacques Servan-Schreiber, one of France's leading magazine publishers, has written a best selling book, The American Challenge, *in which he analyzes what is happening and prescribes a course of action to counter it. How extensive is the American challenge? Why is it alarming? What can be done about it?*

"Will you get rid of De Gaulle," asked President Kennedy in 1963, "or will De Gaulle get rid of you?" The question, addressed to young French publisher Jean-Jacques Servan-Schreiber, was meant only partly as a joke. Even then, Servan-Schreiber was the most eloquent, most influential—and most consistent—critic that *le vieux Charles* had to endure. As a liberal who believed in the West, he abhorred De Gaulle's rejection of the U. S. and Britain as partners in the development of Europe. As publisher of the weekly news magazine *L'Express,* he has constantly attacked Gaullist protectionism as symbolic of "the old France and a petrified Europe." Last week all of France was arguing about a new Servan-Schreiber book that, despite its title, *Le Defi Americain (The American Challenge),* is far more anti-De Gaulle than anti-American.

In the four weeks since it was published, the book has sold 150,000 copies, a French record. It has been reviewed by every reputable French publication. It has been read by practically all the members of the National Assembly and cited by politicians of almost every stripe. . . .

All of Western Europe, says Servan-Schreiber, 43, is being taken over by American industry, which is better organized, more computerized and far more imaginative than anything the Europeans, including France, can produce. Already, the Americans control 50 per cent of European transistor production, 80 per cent of computer production and large percentages of the Continent's heavy industry and oil. In France, U. S. firms produce 65 per cent of agricultural products and telecommunication equipment, 45 per cent of synthetic rubber. Unless Europe wakes up soon, says Servan-Schreiber, "the third industrial power in the world in 15 years, after the U. S. and Russia, could well be not Europe, but American industry in Europe."

Even more alarming to Servan-Schreiber is the fact that 90 per cent of the capital needed to finance this "American invasion" was raised from European investors eager to take part in U. S. ventures. "What threatens us," he writes, "is not a torrent of riches. The war is being fought against us not with dollars, oil, tons of steel or even modern machines, but with creative imagination and a talent for organization." . . . "What America has done is to change the entire concept of culture, the values of civilization. The new American culture is not Chartres or Versailles, but the organization of talent. The Americans organize intelligence so that it creates. They have an industrial and scientific strategy. That's real culture."

What Do You Think?

1.   If you were a European, would you be alarmed or challenged by the American economic penetration?

2.   Do you think the American government should become involved in the "American Challenge"? If so, in what way?

ACTIVITIES FOR INVOLVEMENT

1.   Invite to class a representative from a company that has overseas investments. Ask him to describe what the company is doing overseas and how it justifies its involvement in the business affairs of other countries.

2.   Hold a panel discussion on the topic: Resolved: That foreign companies should be encouraged to establish branches in the United States.

3.   Invite the consul from a European country to discuss with the class his country's feelings about the economic strength and influence that American companies exercise in Europe in general and in his country in particular. Present him with some of the justifications offered by the company representative (see Question 1 above) and ask him to respond.

4.   Have several students do library research and then form a mock panel of economic advisers to the prime minister of a European country to prepare in writing a plan on how to meet the "American Challenge." Describe in the plan the nature, causes, problems, and possible solutions to the challenge.

5.   Hold a debate on the question: Resolved: That American companies should be limited in the amount of investments they may make in Europe. Then hold a series of mock interviews with students portraying the president of General Motors, the president of the A.F.L.-C.I.O., the economic minister of France, and the Secretary of the Treasury of the U.S. to get their reactions to the position which advocates on both sides present.

6.   Write an editorial as it might appear in (a) a European newspaper, and (b) the *Wall Street Journal* on the topic: "U. S. Businessmen on the Move: Beneficial or Harmful?

The Future Role of the United States

You have now examined a sample of America's foreign involvements and some of the implications these provide for the future. This chapter attempts to define the limits of America's role in world affairs. Do world events force our country to intervene in the affairs of other nations? Are there some forms of involvement we should practice and others we should avoid? Is involvement detrimental or beneficial? Can we remain uninvolved in today's world? Here are a number of views for you to consider:

1. PRESIDENT TRUMAN OUTLINES A STRATEGY FOR A BETTER WORLD *

In 1947 President Harry S. Truman suggested the following guidelines for United States involvement in European affairs. Would the present Administration support these ideas?

The peoples of the earth face the future with grave uncertainty, composed almost equally of great hopes and great fears. In this time of doubt they look to the United States, as never before, for good will, strength, and wise leadership. . . .

Since the end of hostilities, the United States has invested its substance and its energy in a great constructive effort to restore peace, stability and freedom to the world. . . .

We have constantly and vigorously supported the United Nations and

---

* Excerpted from Harry S. Truman, Vital Speeches, XV, February 1, 1949.

related agencies as a means of applying democratic principles to international relations. We have consistently advocated and relied upon peaceful settlement of disputes among nations.

We have made every effort to secure agreement on effective international control of our most powerful weapon, and we have worked steadily for the limitation and control of all armaments.

We have encouraged, by precept and example, the expansion of world trade on a sound and fair basis.

Almost a year ago, in company with sixteen free nations of Europe, we launched the greatest cooperative economic program in history. The purpose of that unprecedented effort is to invigorate and strengthen democracy in Europe, so that the free people of that Continent can resume their rightful place in the forefront of civilization and can contribute once more to the security and welfare of the world. . . .

We are moving on with other nations to build an even stronger structure of international order and justice. We shall have as our partners countries which . . . are . . . working to improve the standards of living of all their people. We are ready to undertake new projects to strengthen a free world.

PROGRAM FOR PEACE AND FREEDOM

In the coming years, our program for peace and freedom will emphasize four major courses of action.

First, we will continue to give unfaltering support to the United Nations and related agencies, and we will continue to search for ways to strengthen their authority and increase their effectiveness. We believe that the United Nations will be strengthened by the new nations which are being formed in lands now advancing toward self-government under democratic principles.

Second, we will continue our programs for world economic recovery.

This means, first of all, that we must keep our full weight behind the European Recovery Program. We are confident of the success of this major venture in world recovery. We believe that our partners in this effort will achieve the status of self-supporting nations once again.

In addition, we must carry out our plans for reducing the barriers to world trade and increasing its volume. Economic recovery and peace itself depend on increased world trade.

Third, we will strengthen freedom-loving nations against the dangers of aggression.

We are working out with a number of countries a joint agreement designed to strengthen the security of the North Atlantic area. Such an agreement is within the terms of the United Nations Charter. . . .

The primary purpose of these agreements is to provide unmistakable proof of the joint determination of the free countries to resist armed attack from any quarter. Every country participating in these arrangements must contribute all it can do to the common defense.

If we can make it sufficiently clear, in advance, that any armed attack affecting our national security would be met with overwhelming force, the armed attack might never occur. . . .

In addition, we will provide military advice and equipment to free nations which will cooperate with us in the maintenance of peace and security.

A BOLD NEW PROGRAM

Fourth, we must embark on a bold new program for making the benefits of our scientific advances and industrial progress available for the improvement and growth of under-developed areas.

More than half the people of the world are living in conditions approaching misery. Their food is inadequate. They are victims of disease. Their economic life is primitive and stagnant. Their poverty is a handicap and a threat both to them and to more prosperous areas.

For the first time in history, humanity possesses the knowledge and the skill to relieve the suffering of these people.

The United States is pre-eminent among the nations in the development of industrial and scientific techniques. The material resources which we can afford to use for the assistance of other peoples are limited. But our imponderable resources in technical knowledge are constantly growing and are inexhaustible.

I believe that we should make available to peace-loving peoples the benefits of our store of technical knowledge in order to help them realize their aspirations for a better life. And, in cooperation with other nations, we should foster capital investment in areas needing development.

Our aim should be to help the free peoples of the world, through their own efforts, to produce more food, more clothing, more materials for housing, and more mechanical power to lighten their burdens. The American people desire, and are determined to work for, a world in which all nations and all peoples are free to govern themselves as they see fit and to achieve a decent and satisfying life.

What Do You Think?

1.   How would you describe President Truman's views on foreign policy? What seems to be his strongest point? Weakest?

2.   If Truman were giving this speech today, what parts might be changed? Why?

2.   A HISTORIAN REVIEWS AMERICA'S WORLD ROLE *

In February, 1967, Professor Henry Steele Commager testified before the Senate Foreign Relations Committee during its hearings into "the responsibilities of the United States as a global power." What are those responsibilities?

First I should like to say a word about this matter of the United States as a world power. . . .

The word "power" is an awkward and even a dangerous one for it is used in two ways and it is almost fatally easy to continue the two uses. It is clear that the United States has immense power anywhere on the globe it decides to use it. But it is by no means clear that the United States is, therefore, a world Power—that is spelled, you will note, with a capital P —nor does it follow that we should wish to be such a power.

If you have the strength and do not care overmuch about consequences, it is easy enough to exercise power, but to be a power is a very different thing, and it is a very difficult thing. I do not think the United States is prepared to be a power everywhere—in the Western Hemisphere, in Europe, in Asia—nor do I think we should wish to exercise power everywhere.

There have been in the long course of history, many nations that regarded themselves, and always with some justification, as world powers, but there has never been a nation that could, in fact, exercise power everywhere on the globe. . . .

Because governments must, of necessity, use power, it does not follow that they are capable of using it everywhere or using is absolutely. Our whole history, and our political philosophy, is a monument to the belief that power is limited and that power should be limited. That is, in a sense, what the Revolution itself was about—a repudiation of the British claim . . . that Parliament had the right to bind the colonies and people of America in all cases whatsoever. The American position was, quite simply, that no government had all power. That is part of the meaning of our written constitution—documents which enumerate with greatest care the powers which governments may exercise. That is at the heart of our elaborate system of checks and balances—the determination to limit the authority and the power of government.

That is what the Bill of Rights, state and Federal, are about—limitations on government.

And as Americans have required, and provided, restraint on the domestic scene, so they are pledged to restraint in the international arena. Almost all of our traditions here emphasize limitations on power. The first major principle of American foreign policy was set forth by none other than Washington in the neutrality proclamation, which announced that we were not required to take sides in European wars nor to enter conflicts not of our choosing.

The second and more fundamental principle was the Monroe Doctrine, which was likewise a policy of restraint: Europe was to stay out of the affairs of these Western continents, and we would, in turn, stay out of the internal affairs of Europe. Our third major foreign policy, the Open Door, was likewise designed as a restraint, primarily on ourselves as well.

In . . . the nineties we did find ourselves, somewhat to our own surprise, a world power. We waged a war with Spain that nobody much wanted, and in a fit of absent-mindedness acquired Cuba and Puerto Rico, the Philippines and Hawaii. We fought a three year war with the Filipinos which everyone has pretty well forgotten. But at the same time we repudiated imperialism.

We were not really ready to govern Cuba and very sensibly gave the island back to the Cubans. We did a good job in the Philippines but were eager to get out, and did so. We incorporated Hawaii into the Union and Puerto Rico into the political system and we go before the world with clean hands as it were.

We do not have "colonies." The fact is that we are not very good at the "dominion over palm and pine" sort of thing, and avoid it almost by instinct. And a very good instinct it is.

After 1914 we were unextricably involved in the affairs of Europe— and beyond. But it was President Wilson who called for "peace without victory"—something to remember now. When we had helped win the First World War we did not use victory as a basis for power either in the Old World or in Asia. Indeed, we withdrew far too hastily from our obligations and allowed the League of Nations to sicken and decay.

Although we used something like total power in the Second World War, once victory had been achieved we contented ourselves with trying to put the broken fragments of the war-torn world together again. We used aid, we used influence, we used military power, but we did not use the ultimate power of the nuclear weapon, nor did we in fact attempt to order the affairs of Asia.

It has remained for the statesmen of this decade to insist that we are an Asian power and have the same kind of responsibility for Asia that we have for Western Europe.

It is my feeling that we do not have the resources, material, intellectual or moral, to be at once an American power, a European power, and an Asian power. Justice Holmes used to say that the first lesson a judge had to learn was that he was not God. It is a lesson every man has to learn and a lesson every nation has to learn.

It is not our duty to keep peace throughout the globe, to put down aggression wherever it starts up, to stop the advance of Communism or other isms which we may not approve of. It is primarily the responsibility of the United Nations to keep the peace, to settle disputes, to discourage aggression, and if that organization is not strong enough to do the job, we should perhaps bend our major energies to giving her the necessary authority and the tools.

One explanation of our obsession with Communism and more particularly, now with "Communist aggression" in Asia is to be found . . . in a deep and persistent trait of the American mind: the belief in Old World corruption. The men who won the independence of America from the mother country were convinced that the Old World was abandoned to tyranny, misery, ignorance, injustice and vice, and the New World was innocent of these sins. . . .

The notion of an international Communist conspiracy, which a good many Americans still cling to, fits neatly into this shibboleth of Old World wickedness and New World virtue. And so too, our habit of throwing a mantle of morality over our own wars. We do tend—perhaps more than other nations, to transform our wars into crusades. The Mexican War was part of manifest destiny. The Spanish-American War was a crusade to free Cuba from Spanish tyranny. The First World War was a crusade to make the world safe for democracy. The Second World War did indeed have moral purposes more clearly, I think, than almost any war of modern times.

Our current involvement in Vietnam is cast, increasingly, into a moral mold; it is quite simply, a war to halt Communist aggression.

Closely associated with the notion of New World virtue is the somewhat more activist notion of New World mission. This, too, is a familiar theme: Providence, or history, has put a special responsibility on the American people to spread the blessings of liberty, democracy and equality to other peoples of the world.

What Do You Think?

1. Professor Commager says that the United States has followed a policy of restraint up until World War II, and to some extent, still does. What evidence can you locate to support his contention? Refute it?

2. How might President Truman respond to Professor Commager?

3.   A SENATOR SEEKS AN ECONOMIC UNION OF THE AMERICAS *

In April, 1965, New York's Senator Jacob Javits sent a letter to The New York Times *advocating support for an economic union of the Latin American republics and the United States. Why should the Latin American republics want an economic tie with their northern neighbor?*

The creation of a Latin-American common market (editorial April 22) leading toward the eventual creation of a Western Hemisphere free trade area, including the United States and Canada, is an arrangement which I first proposed in Santiago, Chile, in March 1964; to translate this idea into reality will produce a mass market of some 220 million people with a combined gross national product of between $70 and $80 billion.

The question now is whether there exists the broad public support and political will that are essential to translate proposals of such sweeping nature into action. The critical problem in Latin America today is not a failure of understanding as to what is the answer to the hemisphere's economic and social problems, but the marshaling of the necessary political support to translate this understanding into effective action. It must be made clear also that the development of the Americas requires hemispheric action and not action by Latin America alone.

It is for this reason that I have proposed the formation of an action committee for the economic union of the Americas. Under this proposal leaders of democratic political parties and trade unions of the Americas—which excludes the extremist right and the Communist left—and Latin-American personalities devoted to the cause of democratic reform and unity would join in the establishment of an action committee. This would dedicate its heart and soul and its influence to bringing about a true continental economic union by rallying strong political and public support behind the idea, first, of a treaty for a Latin-American common market composed of all the nations of Latin America, to be followed in due course, as the Latin-American members agree, by a treaty for the Western Hemisphere free trade area.

The committee I proposed . . . would derive its strength from a membership of outstanding distinction in the Americas, largely nongovernmental, agreed on the necessity of achieving the goal of a continental economic union, and committed to influence their respective parliaments, trade unions, and public opinion in general, to realize that goal.

---

* Excerpted from *The New York Times,* April 23, 1965. © 1965 by The New York Times Company. Reprinted by permission.

The need for the political leadership in Latin-American economic and political unification is becoming clearer daily to the governments and people of the hemisphere.

What Do You Think?

The point about American intervention is not that America does in fact interfere in other countries' affairs, but *how* and *why* she does. Would you agree? Explain.

4. PRESIDENT NIXON EXPLAINS HIS FOREIGN POLICY *

In February, 1969, President Nixon visited some of Europe's leaders, to reach a better understanding with them on America's foreign policy. After his return to Washington the President told a press conference that a new confidence and trust between the United States and Europe was developing because of his trip. Is such a new confidence emerging?

We can also say that, as a result of this trip, the United States has indicated its continuing support of the Alliance—the Atlantic Alliance—and that we have also indicated our support of the concept and ideal of European unity.

In addition, we have indicated that we recognize our limitations insofar as European unity is concerned. Americans cannot unify Europe. Europeans must do so. And we should not become involved in differences among Europeans in which our vital interests are not involved. . . .

Sometimes we become rather disillusioned with our aid programs around the world, and we look back on our relations with Europe, particularly, and wonder if it was really worth all that we did immediately after World War II, in terms of the Marshall Plan and other programs.

Anyone who saw Europe as I did in that period of devastation after World War II—when I visited all the countries except Belgium, at that time, that I visited on this trip—and then saw it today, would realize that it was worth doing, because today a strong, prosperous, free Europe stands there, partly a result of our aid.

It could not have happened without our aid. It also, of course, could not have happened without their great efforts on their own behalf. And so, with that recognition, we now realize that this Alliance deserves our atten-

---

* Excerpted from "Launching a New Diplomacy: Nixon's Report to the Nation," *U. S. News & World Report,* March 17, 1969. Copyright 1969 U. S. News & World Report, Inc.

tion, should be the center of our concern, should not be taken for granted. It will not be. That will be a major objective of this Administration. . . .

(Q) Mr. President, . . . what is the policy of your Administration about the carving out of new commitments to other countries by the United States?

The President: Well, I think as far as commitments are concerned, the United States has a full plate. I, first, do not believe that we should make new commitments around the world unless our national interests are very vitally involved. Second, I do not believe we should become involved in the quarrels of nations in other parts of the world unless we are asked to become involved and unless also we are vitally involved. I referred earlier to even the quarrels and divisions in Western Europe. I stayed out of most of those up to this point, and I intend to in the future.

(Q) Mr. President, there were some interpretations some weeks ago of some of General De Gaulle's actions as his wanting to have Western Europe free of American influence. Did he address himself to this in talking with you?

The President: . . . He [General De Gaulle] believes that Europe should have an independent position in its own right. And, frankly, I believe that, too. I think most Europeans believe that. I think the time when it served our interest to have the United States as the dominant partner in an alliance—that that time is gone.

But we will be dominant because of our immense nuclear power and also because of our economic wealth. But on the other hand, the world will be a much safer place and, from our standpoint, a much healthier place economically, militarily and politically if there were a strong European community to be a balance, basically—a balance between the United States and the Soviet Union—rather than to have this polarization of forces in one part of the world or another.

What Do You Think?

1. Is President Nixon's position closer to that of the Monroe Doctrine, President Truman, or Professor Commager? Explain.

2. How would you describe President Nixon's position with regard to involvement? In what way is this position similar, or different, from the policy the United States has followed since World War II? (Refer to Chapter 2, if necessary.)

5.   ISOLATION OR INVOLVEMENT? *

Exactly three months after the press conference shown in part in the last reading, President Nixon was the featured speaker at the Air Force Academy's commencement exercises. He spoke of "America's Role in the World." Would you support such a role as outlined here?

What is America's role in the world? What are the responsibilities of a great nation toward protecting freedom beyond its shores? Can we ever be left in peace if we do not actively assume the burden of keeping the peace?

When great questions are posed, fundamental differences of opinion come into focus. It serves no purpose to gloss over these differences or to try to pretend that they are mere matters of degree.

Because there is one school of thought that holds that the road to understanding with the Soviet Union and Communist China lies through a downgrading of our own alliances and what amounts to a unilateral reduction of our own arms—in order to demonstrate our "good faith."

They believe that we can be conciliatory and accommodating only if we do not have the strength to be otherwise. They believe America will be able to deal with the possibility of peace only when we are unable to cope with the threat of war.

Those who think that way have grown weary of the weight of free-world leadership that fell upon us in the wake of World War II. They argue that we, the United States, are as much responsible for the tensions in the world as the adversaries we face.

They assert that the United States is blocking the road to peace by maintaining its military strength at home and its defenses abroad. If we would only reduce our forces, they contend, tensions would disappear and the chances for peace would brighten. America's powerful military presence on the world scene, they believe, makes peace abroad improbable and peace at home impossible.

Now, we should never underestimate the appeal of the isolationist school of thought. Their slogans are simplistic and powerful: "Charity begins at home. Let's first solve our problems at home and then we can deal with the problems of the world."

This simple formula touches a responsive chord with many an over-burdened taxpayer. It would be easy for the President of the United States

---

* Excerpted from "America's Role in the World," *Department of State Bulletin,* June 23, 1969.

to buy some popularity by going along with the new isolationists. But I submit to you that it would be disastrous for our nation.

I hold a totally different view of the world, and I come to a different conclusion about the direction America must take.

Imagine, for a moment, what would happen to this world if America were to become a dropout in assuming the responsibility for defending peace and freedom in the world. As every world leader knows and as even the most outspoken critics of America would admit, the rest of the world would live in terror. Because, if America were to turn its back on the world, there would be peace that would settle over this planet, but it would be the kind of peace that suffocated freedom in Czechoslovakia.[1]

The danger to us has changed, but it has not vanished. We must revitalize our alliances, not abandon them.

We must rule out unilateral disarmament, because in the real world it wouldn't work. If we pursue arms control as an end in itself, we will not achieve our end. The adversaries in the world are not in conflict because they are armed. They are armed because they are in conflict and have not yet learned peaceful ways to resolve their conflicting national interests.

The aggressors of this world are not going to give to the United States a period of grace in which to put our domestic house in order, just as the crisis within our society cannot be put on a back burner until we resolve the problem of Vietnam.

The most successful solutions that we can possibly imagine for our domestic programs will be meaningless if we are not around to enjoy them. . . . There is no advancement for Americans at home in a retreat from the world. I say that America has a vital national interest in world stability, and no other nation can uphold that interest for us.

What Do You Think?

1.   Were President Nixon's views here compatible with what he said at his press conference three months earlier? If not, why would he change?

2.   Which position do you think is more conducive to bringing world peace: The United States should unilaterally reduce her arms, to demonstrate "good faith" and set an example for other nations to follow, or, the United States should maintain a strong military to discourage would-be aggressors? Defend your views.

---

[1] In August, 1968, a reformist communist government in Czechoslovakia was overthrown by Russian armed forces.

6. BEYOND VIETNAM *

Since resigning from his United Nations post, former Ambassador Arthur Goldberg has often spoken on America's foreign policy. On May 24, 1968, he addressed the National Press Club in Washington, D. C., and discussed a new approach to foreign affairs. How would you compare this approach with the policies of the past twenty-five years?

[S]ome of those who discuss our foreign policy today point to our tragic frustrations in Viet-Nam and conclude that we Americans should give up trying to act like a world power, should return to isolationism, and turn our eyes inward as we did between the two World Wars. I find no merit in that view. Our size, our resources, our technology, our ideals —all these combine to make us a world power and to give us commensurate responsibilities. Our actions abroad, and those of others, have the profoundest consequences for American national security, and it is only realistic to face this fact.

But the same realism also requires us to remember that our national power, great as it is, is not unlimited and that our interests and responsibilities are not unlimited either. Our power does not permit, nor do our interests require, that we directly involve ourselves in every problem that may have international repercussions. America has no choice but to be a world power, but it is under no compulsion to be a world policeman. President Kennedy put his finger on this point when he said:

[T]he United States is neither omnipotent nor omniscient . . . we cannot impose our will . . . we cannot right every wrong or reverse each adversity . . . there cannot be an American solution for every world problem.

As we look beyond Viet-Nam, therefore, we should begin by rejecting the illusion of isolation in a fortress America, and the opposite illusion of an America that is all-powerful and all-wise. We must follow a course that lies between isolationism and interventionism. We must stay on the sensible middle ground—that of a great and responsible world power whose foreign policy seeks to foster a world environment congenial to our historic national purpose of "Life, Liberty, and the pursuit of Happiness." In pursuit of that unchanging aim, our task now is to reappraise those American foreign policies which, in many cases, were conceived to meet circumstances that have changed or are rapidly changing.

---

* Excerpted from "Beyond Vietnam," *Department of State Bulletin,* July 1, 1968.

My own appraisal leads me to the conviction that the course of policy promising the greatest benefits in the near future both for our own national interests and for the peace of the world would be to pursue a *détente* [1] with the Soviet Union and its Eastern European allies and to begin to seek a *modus vivendi* [2] with mainland China. These results will not be achieved solely by our action. But they will certainly not be achieved without our action. . . .

[I]n our search for *détente*, we must begin to reassess European policics born of the cold war. We should seek sensible and practical mutual reductions of troop levels and armaments deployed in Europe by the United States, the Soviet Union, and their respective allies in NATO and the Warsaw Pact. We should seek to eliminate restrictions on trade, travel, and investment between this country and Eastern Europe. We should encourage, and make our contribution to, the growing liberalization of Eastern Europe—being careful, however, not to interfere in ways which could only defeat, rather than accelerate, this trend.

And we should abjure seeking to impose our conception of how Europe should be organized and integrated, but should be content to let the nations of Europe fashion their own future according to their own ideas, as indeed they are in the process of doing. I do not share the fear that those countries, like ourselves, dedicated to democratic ideals, are ready to sacrifice these ideals in this process, in the light of their own experience in the past generation.

In all that we do in search of *détente* in Europe, we should continue to be alert to the possibility that apparent changes in Soviet policy in that area may prove to be only changes in the weather rather than enduring changes in the climate. Therefore we should not be too hasty to abandon alliances that have proved their value, however much they may need to be reviewed in the light of changing circumstances. . . .

In Asia, we must seek new ways—without abandoning old friends— to bring about a relaxation of the hostility between mainland China and ourselves, and most other Asian nations. We can best contribute toward that end by supporting the desires of most Asian countries to achieve— primarily by their own individual and regional efforts—greater security, stability, and growth. With this goal in mind, we should give our help and encouragement to those Asian nations that show the will and capacity not only to remain independent but also to take on an ever-increasing share of responsibility for the security, stability, and growth of the region.

The same general goal should guide our policies in other areas of the world, particularly in Latin America and Africa. In Latin America, the United States has a particular responsibility, rooted in geography and in a

---

[1] a relaxation of strained relations
[2] a practical arrangement that bypasses difficulties

long tradition of good neighborliness, which impels us to continue to extend and to enhance this type of cooperation. . . .

I would not be true to my convictions if I did not add that we must, for our own survival, look much further than this. Even a true *détente* with the Soviet Union, and a *modus vivendi* with mainland China, though greatly to be desired and worth the great efforts involved, would not be the ultimate solution of the difficulties of our world.

A wise American and a former colleague of mine at the United Nations, Ambassador Charles Yost, in his book, "The Insecurity of Nations," has written: "The nature of the modern world is such that it will not tolerate a pax Romana, pax Britannica, pax Sovietica or pax Americana." I would presume to expand his list by adding that the nations of the world would also not long tolerate a pax Americana-Sovietica. And even if they would, the American people would not. Our own revolutionary ideals—our dedication to the right of all men to fashion their own lives—would not permit us to seek to impose peace and stability on the rest of the world, either alone or in conjunction with any other power.

I profoundly believe that nations, including our own, will never know real security until they acknowledge some impartial and effective international agency designed to keep the peace, control national armaments, negotiate peaceful settlements, advance human rights, and facilitate social and economic progress.

It must be acknowledged that the United Nations is not yet such an agency; thus far the members lack the common will to make it so. But despite its weaknesses it is still the best instrument for peace among nations that the world possesses. There is no realistic alternative to it. Our country, in its own interest, cannot afford to slacken its support of this world organization which is so much our own creation or to diminish our efforts to make it more effective.

What Do You Think?

What does Mr. Goldberg mean: "We must follow a course that lies between isolationism and interventionism"? How would you define such a course?

7. CONSTRUCTIVE INITIATIVES FOR FREEDOM AND PEACE *

Some people believe that the products of poverty—disease, ignorance, and famine—present the greatest threat to mankind in the latter part

---

* Excerpted from "Constructive Initiatives for Freedom and Peace," *Department of State Bulletin,* May 13, 1968.

*of the Twentieth Century. Hubert Humphrey, Vice-President of the
United States from 1965 to 1969, here offers suggestions on how the
United States can improve the lives of the people of the world.*

Through affirmative action to meet human needs, we can build security and peace.

Today we seek peace in Asia.

I look forward to the day when all the peoples of Southeast Asia will be participants and partners in economic development and will share in the aid we are able to offer.

I look forward to the day when the great Chinese people, no longer victimized from within, take their place in the modern world. Surely, one of the most exciting and enriching experiences to which we can look forward is the building of peaceful bridges to the people of mainland China. I believe the power of the free idea will in time infiltrate mainland China, as it has infiltrated and is infiltrating the Soviet Union and Eastern Europe.

There will be frustrations. We shall be rebuffed, no doubt, time and again. But we must keep trying. For continued national isolation breeds growing national neurosis—in China as elsewhere.

ACHIEVING CONTROL OF NUCLEAR WEAPONS

Among our highest priorities as we look ahead is achieving greater control over weapons of mass destruction and taking steps that lead us away from the madness of the arms race.

A JOINT ASSAULT ON WANT

. . . We see clear evidence, on all sides, that poverty and injustice in even the most remote nation can lead to the small disorder which causes the large conflict which spreads to the major conflagration which can engulf all of us.

And we see—indeed, as in our own America—that people living trapped and impoverished in a wider society of mobility and affluence are easy victims of demogoguery, incitement, and hate.

We have been trying to deal with this challenge. Through their own efforts, and with some outside help, the developing nations *are* finding their feet. They *are* producing more food and more goods.

And we *are* beginning to learn. We *are* beginning to transform the old and uncomfortable giver-receiver relationship into a joint assault on a mutual enemy—want—wherever it exists. The innovations and experiments of recent years *do* point the way for the future:

· family planning, but on a scale many times larger than what is now being considered;

· overwhelming emphasis in the developing nations—and in our assistance programs—on food production and the building of agricultural infrastructure;

· worldwide commodity agreements which stabilize prices enough so that the producing nations may have at least an even chance of earning their own way;

· international agreements and guarantees to produce a manifold increase in the flow of constructive private investment to the developing nations;

· multilateralism in aid programs along with a limited amount of funds for bilateral use in emergencies;

*   *   *   *   *

· the unleashing of our scientific and technological knowledge about our own earth that we can gain from our new capabilities in space;

· the use of the transistor radio and communications satellite, which can bring 21st century skills and education to even the most remote rural villager;

· the steady removal of barriers to trade among the prosperous nations and the establishment of a global preference system for the goods of the underdeveloped.

These constructive initiatives are the nutrients of freedom and peace. They are the things we Americans must be ready to do if we hope to keep our nation safe and free in a world of growth and change, rather than threatened and isolated in a world of strife.

A secure world, with past differences reconciled, in which men can determine their own destinies, a world free of nuclear peril, a world without starvation and poverty, a world in control of science, not victimized by it—these are objectives worthy of a great people. Are they beyond our power to achieve?

We shall never know unless we try. And try we must, with perseverance and determination.

Whether we like it or not, we live in a world so intricately interdependent that the possibility of withdrawal or isolation simply does not exist.

What Do You Think?

1.   Why should the United States embark upon the program Mr. Humphrey outlines before solving its own domestic problems?

2.   Do private American investments in foreign economic enterprises fit in with Mr. Humphrey's plan? Would the Peace Corps? Explain.

8.   AMERICA FIRST *

Colonel Charles Lindbergh, world-renowned as the first man to fly the Atlantic non-stop, was in 1940 an outspoken advocate of isolationism. He believed America should keep out of the war then going on in Europe. Is there a possibility we may return to this philosophy?

There is a policy open to this nation that will lead to success—a policy that leaves us free to follow our own way of life, and to develop our own civilization. It is not a new and untried idea. It was advocated by Washington. It was incorporated in the Monroe Doctrine. Under its guidance, the United States has become the greatest nation in the world.

It is based upon the belief that the security of a nation lies in the strength and character of its own people. It recommends the maintenance of armed forces sufficient to defend this hemisphere from attack by any combination of foreign powers. It demands faith in an independent American destiny. . . . It is a policy not of isolation, but of independence; not of defeat, but of courage. It is a policy that led this nation to success during the most trying years of our history, and it is a policy that will lead us to success again.

We have weakened ourselves for many months, and, still worse, we have divided our own people by this dabbling in Europe's wars. While we should have been concentrating on American defense, we have been forced to argue over foreign quarrels. We must turn our eyes and our faith back to our own country before it is too late. And when we do this, a different vista opens before us. Practically every difficulty we would face in invading Europe becomes an asset to us in defending America. Our enemy, and not we, would then have the problem of transporting millions of troops across the ocean and landing them on a hostile shore. They, and not we, would have to furnish the convoys to transport guns and trucks and munitions and fuel across three thousand miles of water. Our battleships and our submarines would then be fighting close to their home bases. We would then do the bombing from the air and the torpedoing at sea. And if any part of an enemy convoy should ever pass our Navy and our Air Force, they would still be faced with the guns of our coast artillery and behind them the divisions of our Army.

The United States is better situated from a military standpoint than any other nation in the world. Even in our present condition of unpreparedness no foreign power is in a position to invade us today. If we

---

* Excerpted from *The New York Times,* April 24 and 30, 1941. © 1941 by The New York Times Company. Reprinted by permission.

concentrate on our own defenses and build the strength that this nation should maintain, no foreign army will ever attempt to land on American shores.

What Do You Think?

Would Colonel Lindbergh's plan be feasible today? Who might support it? Oppose it?

9. A POLITICAL COMMENTATOR ASKS, "WHAT CAN WE DO?" *

Dan Smoot is a former F.B.I. agent who became a political commentator. He is best known for his radio program, "Dan Smoot Reports." Smoot believes that America faces dangers and that her security is in jeopardy. What are these dangers? What can be done about them?

For sixteen years we have seen the disastrous fallacy of trying to handle the foreign affairs of our great nation through international agencies. This leaves us without a policy of our own, and makes it impossible for us to take any action in our own interest or against the interests of communism, because communists have more actual votes, and infinitely more influence, in all the international agencies than we have. At the same time, our enemies, the communist nations, set and follow their own policies, contemptuously ignoring the international agencies which hamstring America and bleed American taxpayers for subsidies to our mortal enemies.

America must do two things soon if she expects to survive as a free and independent nation:

(1) We must withdraw from membership in all international, governmental, or quasi-governmental organizations — including, specifically, the World Court, the United Nations, and all UN specialized agencies. (2) We must act vigorously, unilaterally, and quickly, to protect vital American security interests in the Western Hemisphere—particularly in Cuba.

We have already passed the time when we can act in Cuba easily and at no risk; but if we have any sane, manly concern for protecting the vital security of the American nation and the lives and property of United States citizens, we had better do the only thing left for us to do: send overwhelming American military force to take Cuba over quickly, and keep

---

* Excerpted from Dan Smoot, *The Invisible Government,* Belmont, Mass.: Western Islands, 1968.

it under American military occupation, as beneficently as possible, until the Cuban people can hold free elections to select their own government.

*   *   *   *   *

WHAT SHOULD WE DO ABOUT BERLIN?

Berlin will cause a world war only when the United States is willing to go to war with the Soviet Union to free Berlin from the trap it is in.[1] If we won't defend our own vital interests against the aggressive and arrogant actions of communists 90 miles from our shores, what would prompt us to cross the ocean and defend Germans from communists?

The cold fact of the matter is that we should not defend Berlin. This is a job for Germans, not Americans.

The Germans are an able and prosperous people. They are capable of fighting their own war if war is necessary to protect them from communism.

What part should we play? We should do exactly what the President[2] and the State Department assure the world they will not do: we should present the Soviets with a *fait accompli,* and an ultimatum.

We should call an immediate conference with the governments of France, England, and West Germany to explain that America has devoted 16 years and many billions of dollars to rehabilitating and defending Western Europe; that Europe is now in many ways more soundly prosperous than we are; that the 180 million Americans can no longer be expected to ruin their own economy and neglect the defense of their own homeland for the purpose of assisting and defending the 225 million people of Western Europe; and that, therefore, we are through.

We have no need, at home, for all of the vast stores of military equipment which we now have in Europe for the defense of Europe. What we do not need for the defense of our homeland, we should offer as a gift to West Germany, since we produced the material in the first place for the purpose of resisting communism, and since the West Germans are the only people in Western Europe who apparently want to resist it.

We should give the West Germans (and the other western powers) six months to train whatever manpower they want for manning their own defenses. At the end of that time, we should pull out and devote ourselves to defending America.

---

[1] Berlin lies inside East Germany.
[2] President Kennedy

What Do You Think?

1. Mr. Smoot says that in Europe we should present Russia with a *fait accompli* and an ultimatum. How does this view differ from Mr. Goldberg's idea on how to deal with Russia? Which position would you endorse and why?
2. Some individuals have argued that the United States should withdraw her troops from all foreign countries *immediately*. How would you respond to this view? Explain.

10. IS UNCLE SAM "OVEREXTENDED"? *

In this article it is suggested that the United States has done much for the world, but has received little gratitude for its efforts. What do you think?

In many ways Uncle Sam has never looked healthier or more prosperous than he does today. He presides over the most robustly productive economy the world has ever seen. He is widely recognized as the strongest power in the world community in which he lives. To some degree, large or small, his presence is felt in just about every region of the globe.

Yet the face that Uncle Sam turns to the world in 1968 does not seem to wear an expression of self-confidence. In truth, Uncle Sam is suffering from an assortment of aches and pains: a throbbing headache called Viet Nam, heartburn in his urban regions, and a rundown feeling from living with one crisis after another. And for these, no "miracle ingredients" have appeared to promise fast! Fast! FAST! relief.

Some, indeed, fear that Uncle Sam is suffering from spiritual fatigue. For more than 20 years now, he has shouldered the main burden of guarding the non-Communist world. He has been a generous benefactor to a needy world, dispensing some $130 billion worth of foreign aid to date. While he has undoubtedly made mistakes, he sincerely believes that, on the whole, he has exerted a positive influence on the maintenance of worldwide stability.

But often to his dismay he senses that his efforts are not universally applauded or even appreciated. Many of his policies, in fact, have undergone sharp criticism—not only from his enemies but also from those he had considered his closest friends. And frankly, Uncle Sam's feelings are pretty sensitive and his pride may be hurt.

---

* "Is Uncle Sam 'Overextended'?", *Senior Scholastic,* April 4, 1968. Reprinted by permission of Scholastic Magazines, Inc. © 1968 Scholastic Magazines, Inc.

In the sense that Uncle Sam is a symbol of this American nation, this imaginary description of Uncle Sam's current state of affairs may be taken as a symbol of the current mood of the U. S. public. It seems to be a mood characterized by frustration, a sense of disappointment that our massive involvement in global affairs has not produced the kind of world that we would really like. This, in turn, creates new doubts—a feeling that we as a nation must be doing something wrong.

To a large measure, this sense of uneasiness is a direct offshoot of the heated national debate over the Viet Nam war. Examining the complex questions surrounding that war has become almost a full-time occupation in itself. Still, Viet Nam is not entirely an isolated problem that suddenly plopped into the laps of U. S. policymakers. No meaningful probing of the problem can be complete without some attempt to relate Viet Nam to the over-all aims and problems of U. S. foreign policy. If anything, the painfulness of the Viet Nam experience has added a sense of urgency to calls for a broad reassessment of U. S. foreign policy goals.

Has the U. S. as some foreign policy critics have charged, put itself into the role of "policeman to the world"? These critics say that the U. S. has gotten into a habit of dashing breathlessly around the world, jumping into every big and little crisis that comes along, all in the name of maintaining world peace and tranquility. They question whether any one nation, no matter how strong it may be, can successfully correct all of the world's troubles all by itself. By trying to do too much in too many places, they argue, the U. S. has dangerously overextended its own energy and resources.

What Do You Think?

1. "Often to his dismay," Uncle Sam "senses that his efforts are not universally applauded or even appreciated." Do the recipients of financial and military aid owe gratitude to the United States? Should we continue to help others if they do not show gratitude?

2. If the United States does not act as the world's policeman, who will? What would be the world's future if there were no policeman?

ACTIVITIES FOR INVOLVEMENT

1. Write a letter from Arthur Goldberg to:
    a. President Kennedy on the Peace Corps.
    b. Vice-President Humphrey about his views on economic development.
    c. Secretary McNamara on Vietnam.
    d. Senator Javits on his economic union idea.

2.   Stage a panel discussion between President Truman, Professor Commager, Dan Smoot, and President Nixon on America's role in Europe today. You will have to do more research on their ideas.
(See the *Reader's Guide to Periodical Literature, The New York Times* Index, and the card catalog in the library.)

3.   Study the foreign policy planks of the Democratic and Republican parties' 1968 platforms.

   a. Comment on them from Professor Commager's viewpoint.

   b. Comment on them from your viewpoint.

4.   Write a program for the United States, as one of the two leading countries of the world, to follow in Asia, Africa, Latin America, and Europe. Divide your class into four groups, one for each area. After each group completes its program, have it report to the entire class and have a discussion. After the discussion, let each group rewrite its report, incorporating the ideas it accepts from the class. Finally, to give additional worth to your work, make arrangements to present your final reports to another class studying American foreign policy.

5.   Professor Commager says: "It is clear that the United States has immense power anywhere on the globe it decides to use it. But it is by no means clear that the United States is, therefore, a world Power—that is spelled, you will note, with a capital P—nor does it follow that we should wish to be such a power." Divide your class into groups of five or six students each. Discuss Commager's definition of power. Do you accept it? Then discuss whether you believe the United States is a global power. Have a group leader and a secretary in each case. After the group discussions, have the secretaries report each group's thought to the whole class. Let the class then discuss the secretaries' reports.

6.   Which of the words below best describe America's foreign policy? Least describes it? Why?

defender of democracy	selfish	bully
liberator	egotistical	meddler
aggressor	ethnocentric	humanitarian
helpful	sacrificing	exploiter
political manipulator	self-defense	

Would you add any words to the list?

7.   Write a brief paper in which you express how you think each of the following would describe the kind of foreign policy America needs today:

   a. Richard Nixon

   b. Henry Steele Commager

   c. Harry S. Truman

   d. Arthur Goldberg

   e. Your own parents

8.   Write a song or a poem on some aspect of America's foreign policy.

BIBLIOGRAPHY
For Further Study

BIBLIOGRAPHY
For Further Study

Books

BEMIS, SAMUEL F. · *American Foreign Policy and the Blessings of Liberty and Other Essays* · New Haven, Conn.: Yale University Press, 1962.

BINGHAM, JONATHAN B. · *Shirt-Sleeve Diplomacy: Point 4 in Action* · New York, N. Y.: The John Day Company, Inc., 1954.

BRAEBNER, NORMAN A. · *Empire on the Pacific; A Study in American Continental Expansion* · New York, N. Y.: The Ronald Press Company, 1955.

COLE, WAYNE S. · *America First, The Battle Against Intervention, 1940–1941* · Madison, Wis.: Univ. of Wisconsin Press, 1953.

DANIELS, JOSEPHUS · *Shirt-Sleeve Diplomat* · Chapel Hill, N. C.: Univ. of North Carolina Press, 1947.

DULLES, FOSTER RHEA · *The Imperial Years* · New York, N. Y.: Thomas Crowell Company, 1956.

DULLES, JOHN FOSTER · *War or Peace* · New York, N. Y.: The Macmillan Company, 1957.

FERRARA, ORESTES · *The Last Spanish War* · New York, N. Y.: Paisley Press, 1937.

FREIDEL, FRANK · *The Splendid Little War* · Boston, Mass.: Little, Brown & Company, 1958.

GOODRICH, LELAND · *A Study of U. S. Policy in the United Nations* · New York, N. Y.: Council on Foreign Relations, 1956.

KENNAN, GEORGE F. · *Realities of American Foreign Policy* · Princeton, N. J.: Princeton Univ. Press, 1954.

KENNEDY, ROBERT F. · *Thirteen Days: A Memoir of the Cuban Missile Crisis* · New York, N. Y.: W. W. Norton & Company, 1969.

KISSINGER, HENRY A. · *Nuclear Weapons and Foreign Policy* · New York, N. Y.: Harper & Row, 1957.

LENS, SIDNEY · *The Futile Crusade; Anti-Communism as American Credo* · Chicago, Ill.: Quadrangle Books, 1964.

MEYER, KARL and SZULC, TAD · *The Cuban Invasion: The Chronicle of a Disaster* · New York, N. Y.: Frederick Praeger, Publisher, 1962.

PERKINS, DEXTER · *Hands Off: A History of the Monroe Doctrine* · Boston, Mass.: Little, Brown & Company, 1941.

SCHESINGER, ARTHUR M., JR. · *A Thousand Days: John F. Kennedy in the White House* · Boston, Mass.: Houghton Mifflin Company, 1965.

SORENSEN, THEODORE C. · *Kennedy* · New York, N. Y.: Harper & Row, Publishers, 1965.

SULZBERGER, C. L. · *What's Wrong with U. S. Foreign Policy* · New York, N. Y.: Harcourt, Brace and World, Inc., 1959.

WEINBERG, ALBERT · *Manifest Destiny: A Study of National Expansionism in American History* · Baltimore, Md.: Johns Hopkins Press, 1935.

WISAN, JOSEPH · *The Cuban Crisis as Reflected in the New York Press, 1895–1898* · New York, N. Y.: Columbia Univ. Press, 1934.

WISE, DAVID and ROSS, THOMAS · *The Invisible Government* · New York, N. Y.: Random House, 1964.

Paperback Books

ADLER, S. · *Isolationist Impulse: Its Twentieth Century Reaction* · New York, N. Y.: Free Press.

BAIN, CHESTER A. · *Vietnam: The Roots of Conflict* · Englewood Cliffs, N. J.: Spectrum Books, Prentice-Hall, Inc.

CORDIER, ANDREW and FOOTE, WILDER (eds.) · *Quest for Peace* · New York, N. Y.: Columbia Univ. Press.

DOZER, D. · *Monroe Doctrine: Its Modern Significance* · New York, N. Y.: Alfred Knopf.

DULLES, FOSTER R. · *Imperial Years* · New York, N. Y.: Apollo Editions.

FIFIELD, RUSSELL · *Southeast Asia in U. S. Policy* · New York, N. Y.: Frederick A. Praeger, Inc.

FUENTES, CARLOS, et al. · *Whither Latin America* · Monthly Review Press.

HICKEY, GERALD · *Village in Vietnam* · New Haven, Conn.: Yale Univ. Press.

HICKERMAN, LEO and SWEEZY, PAUL · *Cuba: Anatomy of a Revolution* · Monthly Review Press.

HUMPHREY, HUBERT · *Cause Is Mankind: A Liberal Program for Modern America* · Macfadden-Bartell Corp.

KENNAN, GEORGE F. · *American Diplomacy: 1900–1950* · Chicago, Ill.: Univ. of Chicago Press, 1951.

MAY, E. R. · *American Intervention, 1917 and 1941* · Service Center For History Teachers.

MERK, F. · *Manifest Destiny and Mission in American History* · New York, N. Y.: Random House.

OSBORN, ROBERT · *Mankind May Never Make It* · New York Graphic Society (Time-Life Corp.).

PADDOCK, WILLIAM and PAUL · *Hungry Nations* · Boston, Mass.: Little, Brown & Co.

PERKINS, DEXTER · *Evaluation of American Foreign Policy* · New York, N. Y.: Oxford Univ. Press.

ROSS, HUGH · *Cold War: Containment and Its Critics* · Chicago, Ill.: Rand McNally & Co.

Articles

"Ambassadors of Good Will," *National Geographic Magazine,* CXXVI, September, 1964.

BAILEY, THOMAS · "America's Emergence As a World Power: The Myth and the Verity," *Pacific Historical Review,* XXX, 1961.

CURTI, MERLE, E. · "Young America," *American Historical Review,* XXXII, October, 1926.

DOOLEY, THOMAS · "The Edge of Tomorrow," *Reader's Digest,* LXXII, May, 1958.

DOOLEY, THOMAS · "The Night They Burned The Mountain," *Reader's Digest,* LXXVI, May, 1960.

"Five Thousand Years Older than San Claus," *Harper's,* CXIII, August, 1956.

HARRINGTON, FRED · "The Anti-Imperialist Movement in the United States, 1898–1900," *Mississippi Valley Historical Review,* XXII, September, 1935.

"International Law, Morality, and American Intervention," *Catholic World,* CCI, September, 1965.

MCGEE, GALE, W. · "The Monroe Doctrine: A Stopgap Measure," *Mississippi Valley Historical Review,* XXXVIII, 1951.

"My Life as a Peace Corps Girl," *Good Housekeeping,* CLVIII, April, 1963.

"Mysterious Doings of the C. I. A.," *Saturday Evening Post,* CCXXVII, October 30, 1954, pp. 19ff; November 6, 1954; November 13, 1954.

PERKINS, DEXTER · "Bringing the Monroe Doctrine Up to Date," *Foreign Affairs,* XX, January, 1942.

PRATT, JULIUS · "The Origin of 'Manifest Destiny'," *American Historical Review,* XXII, July, 1927.

RIPPY, J. FRED · "Antecedents of the Roosevelt Corollary of the Monroe Doctrine," *Pacific Historical Review,* IX, September, 1940.

SMITH, BEVERLY · "White House Story: Why We Went to War in Korea," *Saturday Evening Post,* November 10, 1951.

WEIGLE, RICHARD · "Sugar and the Hawaiian Revolution," *Pacific Historical Review,* XIV, February, 1947.

"We Were Betrayed," *U. S. News and World Report,* LIV, January 14, 1963.

"We Who Tried: The Bay of Pigs," *Life,* LIV, May 10, 1963.

"When The Marines Stormed Ashore," *Saturday Evening Post,* CCXXXVIII, July 31, 1965.

Films

Aftermath of World War II—Prologue to the Cold War (25 min; B/W; McGraw-Hill Textfilms) · Shows Allied victory, birth of the U. N., emergence of the U. S. and U. S. S. R. as the Big Two. Discusses nationalism in Asia, divided Germany, the Truman Doctrine, and fear of atomic war.

American Foreign Policy—Confrontation 1945–1953 (31 min; B/W; Encyclopaedia Britannica Films) · Discusses America's role of leadership after World War II, the Truman Doctrine, the Marshall Plan, and NATO. Explains that Korean War challenged America's leadership. Shows problems of avoiding a nuclear war.

American Foreign Policy—Containment in Asia (32 min; B/W; Encyclopaedia Britannica Films) · Shows that the collapse of colonial powers in Asia left the U. S. the only power capable of limiting the spread of communism. Discusses the establishment of SEATO and relations with Japan.

American Foreign Policy—Foundations (30 min; B/W; Encyclopaedia Britannica Films) · Professor Odegard outlines the nature of American foreign policy through its history.

American Foreign Policy—Instrument for Foreign Aid (10 min; B/W; Encyclopaedia Britannica Films) · Explains how the United States, in dispensing aid, hopes to establish strong, independent countries, which will work toward a free society. Discusses how aid can be used as an instrument of foreign policy.

American Foreign Policy—Instrument of Intervention (13 min; B/W; Encyclopaedia Britannica Films) · Shows how the United States' decision to intervene in the Dominican Republic blew up a worldwide storm. Points out previous examples that had similar results and explains American policy of helping threatened people.

America's Relations With Her Neighbors to the South (30 min; Norwood Films) · America's interests in Panama, the Caribbean, and Central America, building hemispheric solidarity.

Colonial Expansion of European Nations (13½ min; color or B/W; Coronet Films) · Why Europeans settled unknown lands during the colonial expansion period of the 16th and 17th Centuries. Empires that resulted from these settlements.

Growth of American Foreign Policy (19 min; B/W; McGraw-Hill Textfilms) · Using charts, maps, and authentic motion pictures, film traces the major steps in the evolution of United States foreign policy from 18th Century isolationism to 20th Century leadership.

The Louisiana Purchase—Key to a Continent (16 min; B/W; Encyclopaedia Britannica Films) ·

The Monroe Doctrine (16 min; United Artists Associated, Inc.) · The Monroe Doctrine from Monroe to Teddy Roosevelt.

The Nation Expands to The Pacific: American (30 min; B/W; Norwood Films) · American frontiers, settlement of the West, acquisition of Texas, annexation of Oregon, and the Mexican War.

The United States Adopts a Policy of Imperialism (30 min; B/W; Norwood Films) · Spanish-American War, peace terms, and acquisition of Spanish possessions, U. S. handling of new territories of Puerto Rico and The Philippines. Traces U.S.-Cuba relations.

The United States Continues Its Policy of Isolation (30 min; Norwood Films) · The United States applies the Monroe Doctrine in Latin America; how the U. S. acquired overseas professions; America's relations with England.

United States Expansion: Florida (14 min; B/W; Coronet Films) · Recounts the history of Florida from discovery to American acquisition. Discusses Andrew Jackson's role in bringing about Florida's annexation.

United States Expansion: The Oregon Country (13½ min; color or B/W; Coronet Films) · Key events in the history of the Oregon Country, Lewis and Clark expedition, subsequent Westward movement, rivalry of the British and American interests, acquisition of the Oregon Territory by the United States.

United States Expansion: Overseas, 1893–1917 (13½ min; color or B/W; Coronet Films) · Reviews United States expansion into Hawaii, Cuba, the Philippines and Latin America. The changing policy from isolationism to world power. Problems of expansion.

The United States in a Revolutionary World (29 min; B/W; Indiana Univ. Audio-Visual Center) · Discusses debates in America since World War I over the issue of isolation versus involvement in world affairs. Reviews our participation in League of Nations, neutrality acts of the 1930's, post-World War II foreign aid, and America's involvement in the Korean War.

1947—Year of Division (20 min; B/W; Teaching Films Custodians, Inc.) · Split between East and West. Russia attempts to dominate the post World War II impoverished nations. The Marshall Plan.

Filmstrips

America Develops World-Wide Interests Series (*American Interests in Asia*, 38 fra; *Island Possessions*, 36 fra; *The Panama Canal*, 29 fra; *The Spanish-American War*, 30 fra; *The United States Joins The Allies*, 32 fra; Eye Gate House) · Covers the period from 1900 to 1920, shows the U. S. emerging as one of the world's greatest powers.

America Fights for Freedom Series (*The Monroe Doctrine Shapes U. S. History*, 40 fra; *The Strategic Panama Canal*, 40 fra; *Texas—The Fight For Independence*, 40 fra; Popular Science Publishing Co.) ·

America's Responsibilities in a Divided World (50 fra; The New York Times, Office of Educational Activities) · Explains the former isolationist policy of the United States and outlines factors which compelled the United

States to take up responsibilities which were inevitable corollaries of economic power.

America's Stake in Asia (57 fra; The New York Times, Office of Educational Activities) · Examines America's growing commitments in a changing Asia.

Mexican Cession and Gadsen Purchase (40 fra; Curriculum Materials Corporation) · How this territory was added to the United States through a process of settlement, revolution, aggression, and purchase.

United States and Its Alliances (54 fra; The New York Times, Office of Educational Activities) · Points out the anti-communist alliances, compares the communist and non-communist countries' economies, and reveals problems among free world allies.

The Universal Declaration of Human Rights (73 fra; Stankow Productions, Inc.) · In graphic form, content and significance of the Universal Declaration of Human Rights. Produced by the U.N.

United States Foreign Policy (53 fra; The New York Times, Office of Educational Activities) · Illustrates American foreign policy aims of supporting freedom and avoiding atomic warfare through support of U.N. Discusses Truman Doctrine, NATO, Atoms For Peace Program, Actions in Europe and Asia.

Tapes

Pacem in Terris: The Pope's Encyclical (7″ diameter spool; 60 min; Center for the Study of Democratic Institutions) · Discussion of Pope John XXIII's encyclical, Pacem in Terris. Its impact on the world. What an encyclical is and is not.